A Culture Turned

USING UGRs TO BOOST PERFORMANCE AND CULTURE

Steve Simpson & Stef du Plessis

ISBN: 1481017659
ISBN 13: 9781481017657
Library of Congress Control Number: 2014911592
CreateSpace Independent Publishing Platform
North Charleston, South Carolina

PRAISE FOR 'A CULTURE TURNED'

Lots of authors talk about the need for culture change within companies; Steve and Stef truly define it. 'A Culture Turned' shows you how to transform your culture – and keep it there.

Kevin Haviland, Vice President, Manager Client Acquisition, Barclays Business Banking, Africa

Writing down the "Unwritten Ground Rules" is like having a magic key to aligning an organisation and its teams with its leaders. Every time I guide my clients to apply this concept, their project results come more easily, happen more quickly, and generally last longer. I think it's because UGRs connect with the people inside the roles. They bring meaning to work and help individuals align with each other more naturally.

Mike Wittenstein, Storyminers, USA

I work as a consultant helping companies improve their supply chain management processes, and I found the UGRs concept to be invaluable in helping me to 'crack the culture code' of my client's organisations

John Fink, Canada

Culture eats strategy for breakfast. Drucker said it, we all know it. And yet so many organisations spend lots on strategy, but often forget or brush over the concept of creating a great culture that allows strategy and execution to succeed. UGRs is an invaluable tool/approach/framework to understanding the things that really matter. Fix these, and you are half-way to successful execution of strategic intent.

Love the concept of UGRs.

Tony Cross, Puzzle Piece Consulting, South Africa

We run a 3 day "Managing People" course specifically contextualised for our industry. At the beginning of day one we get our Managing Director to talk about his vision for our organisation and this is when we introduce culture. We play a YouTube clip of you talking about UGRs and we revisit this concept throughout the 3 days. I find it wonderful because it is straight talk, no spin, and puts the onus of accountability back onto our managers.

Karen Isherwood, Pathology Queensland, Australia

For me, the greatness in the UGRs concept is in its simplicity. It gets to the truth about corporate culture and deals with the real issues. The very concept can be applied in all sorts of situations. Basically, as a manager it tells me to lead by example, it's not what we say but what we actually do that influences others. Around here, people's awareness around culture has been elevated to another level and I am certainly starting to see positive results. It is not a quick fix, and ties in so well with the 'Good to Great' momentum principle. I have no doubt this UGRs concept will take deep root in our organisation and will bear fruit both in people's personal lives and in our corporate workplace for many years to come.

As you can see, I am a massive fan of this concept and try to use it as often as I can.

Steve Poorter, General Manager, Aveng Grinaker, South Africa

As a past Chairperson of the Culture Champion group within a large state Government IT service provider to health I have found the UGRs concept invaluable and often write on the whiteboard sentences such as 'Around here, everyone is given...' It's a great test or confirmation of cultural climate. Love your work.

Kris Johns, Queensland Health, Australia

We have used your UGRs concept extensively in our organisation. We have embedded it into our mandatory training program that staff attend each year and our orientation program for new staff.

The point we have emphasised is that they (the staff) have such a huge impact on the culture and that 'the ball is in their court' in influencing the culture. We are making them aware of it and have had great feedback in doing so.

Michael Penhey, CEO, Parish Aged Care Services, Australia

Our company embarked on this road just over 2 years ago and we continue to see the positive results.

For many of our staff it has become part of their "DNA" where you no longer have to think about certain things, it all happens sub-consciously.

The UGRs program is very easy to understand, a means to truly connect with your staff and a fun way to collaborate, implement and "live" by.

Martin Roets, Operations Director, Rectron, South Africa

Our group undertook a UGRs Stock Take a while back. There is no doubt this comprehensive staff survey became the catalyst for the most detailed review of "the way things were being done around here" which ultimately led to significant changes being initiated across the group.

It is recognised that a strong workplace culture can be the difference between having impressive employee retention rates and high employee satisfaction levels and I am proud to say that our group currently exceeds best practice within our industry.

Gary Butcher, Manager Business Services, Dexar Group, Australia

I have found throughout my years of experience that it is the UGRs that unofficially direct and influence the workplace – often negatively. When the concept is brought to the attention of staff and workplace UGRs are explored, to quote a cliché, "the light comes on."

I find it an invaluable concept in which people easily engage and assists in the process of encouraging individuals to take responsibility for their own actions and behaviours. Cultural change can be so difficult but if UGRs are acknowledged, particularly by leaders and staff can see how they may be contributing or defining UGRs, achieving change can be easier. If leaders embrace analysis of the UGRs – that is, are willing to gain an understanding of why they might exist – and staff can openly express why 'they do what they do', amazing results can be achieved.

Lyndie Spurr, Ex-President, Australian Council of Community Nursing Services Inc.

I read Steve's first UGRs book years ago and use the principles regularly. Earlier in my life, I had committed to absolute integrity and didn't understand why company life was so difficult. I have turned an organisation into being open & honest because of the book.

I counsel and coach managers and recommend that they read the book as part of understanding work dynamics.

Bob Lane, Queensland, Australia

As a long-time subscriber to the UGR newsletters I've found the greater concept of Unwritten Ground Rules and indeed the articles therein valuable in challenging my thinking and evolving my leadership style. Potentially most valuable however is knowing that I'm not alone in many of my challenges!

In short, thanks for the journey and keep up the great work!

Luke Say, Manager Independent Living Services, ECH Inc, Australia

Dedicated to our wives, Lesley-Anne and Maureen

ABOUT THE AUTHORS

*S*teve Simpson

Based in Melbourne, Australia, Steve is an international speaker and culture change agent. He created the one-of-a-kind UGRs concept in the mid-90's, initially focussed on helping companies to understand that without a solid culture - built on UGRs - their efforts to improve service would, at best, be limited.

Steve continues to travel the world, speaking at conferences and working with organisations to help them understand, and strategically improve, their culture. Besides already having achieved the highest accreditation in professional speaking almost a decade earlier, he earned the ultimate accolade for his ground-breaking work spanning five continents when Professional Speakers Australia bestowed on him its coveted 'Educator of the Year Award' in 2015.

Steve has a Masters Degree from the University of Alberta (Canada). He is the author of two books, and the co-author of two more, including 'UGRs: Creating a Culture of Service' and 'The Power of Culture.'

www.steve-simpson.com

Stef du Plessis

It was Stef's prominence in the financial services industry that led to a chance invitation for him to speak at a sales convention back in '92. What was meant to be a one-off thing soon catapulted him on to the stages of premier events around the globe - like the Million Dollar Round Table, branded as the world's premier sales event. Since then, he has delivered thousands of paid presentations, and earned every award and accreditation in professional speaking.

Stef's transition from speaking to organisational development came in three stages. First, when he went back to school at age 40 to earn a Masters Degree in leadership (cum laude) from the University of Johannesburg. Then, when his former professor traded academia to become one his course presenters, culminating in them co-developing a framework for effective employee engagement for some of the world's biggest enterprises. And finally, when he partnered with Steve - and UGRs - around the turn of the century.

Stef has written two books, most recently 'A Culture Turned,' co-authored with Steve. He and his family live in Johannesburg, South Africa.

www.stefduplessis.com

FOREWORD

WHEN WE MET FLEETINGLY AT a conference in Adelaide, Australia in 2001, neither of us knew that that chance meeting would change the lives of each of us, and our families, for ever.

By then, Stef had already emerged as one of South Africa's most influential employee engagement practitioners. Having built a team of a dozen-or-so OD practitioners - each with at least a relevant Masters degree, and even including his former university professor - he led employee engagement programmes for major corporations, most of who employed upward of 10,000 people.

Steve, on the other hand, had by then earned a reputation as one of Australia's leading authorities on customer service. In the few years prior to this chance meeting, he had already started transitioning into the domain of corporate culture (or, as we now prefer to call it: workplace culture), having discovered that service, like virtually all else workplace-related, is in fact driven by culture. He found that when you improve culture, you improve service (as well as just about everything else in the workplace). But he also found that managers generally lacked the insights, and the tools, with which to manage, and improve, culture in the workplace. And so, he set out to find a fix for this gap – in the process creating the concept of Unwritten Ground Rules, or UGRs® (which you'll learn all about in the pages of this book).

By the time that we met, UGRs was already a formidable process, built on the world-first research done by Steve in collaboration with two leading Australian universities (the University of Western Australia, and Curtin University of Technology). And Steve was already using UGRs to help his clients around the globe to improve their results by showing leaders how to really understand, and then manage workplace culture, to a point where they - and their people - could truly create, and sustain, a culture-by-design.

All the while, Stef had been evolving a unique approach to employee engagement under the auspices of the University of Johannesburg, looking for new ways to get employees on board and on track.

As soon as we got a glimpse of each other's body of work, we knew, then and there, that our respective bodies of work were a perfect fit. The fact that we got along from the very first moment that we met was just an added bonus.

Soon after that first meeting, Stef brought Steve in to run a UGRs session with the executive team of one of his key clients, at the time the world's leading gold mining company. Neither of us had any idea that that session would effectively become the launch of our first multi-million dollar contract for this client, ultimately touching some 50,000 employees across a number of countries.

That project was the first of many, and became the genesis of the evolution of the UGRs concept – as well as our business partnership and deep personal friendship. Since then, we have jointly developed the UGRs concept into what it is today: an end-to-end workplace culture transformation solution, which has now been used by organisations in more than 50 countries to crank up - and sustain - their results.

Although we've lived on different continents throughout the entire time that we've known one-another, we collaborate almost daily - sharing insights and comparing research results focussed on improving the impact of UGRs in the workplace.

Our business model is a very simple one: for smaller culture change programmes in organisations based primarily on one country, each of us works independently. When it comes to running UGRs programmes for our many multi-national clients - often spanning across continents - we work together.

In spite of the cliché, real magic happens when we are in front of a room together: be it a boardroom, training room, factory workshop floor or floodlit stage. This, because although we share values, we are different in every other way: experience, competence, field of formal education, personalities that are poles apart and vastly divergent communication styles. Yet, when we are together in front of a room, all this seamlessly gels to create truly unique and transformational learning outcomes.

This book has been years in the making. We say that it is fictional. But that's not 100% accurate, because we've drawn on our experiences working with dozens (upon dozens) of organisations of all sizes - across virtually all industries - in many different countries.

So, the storyline in this book, namely the company's culture profile, the character types and traits of its people and their conversations are based on the many real-life experiences that we've encountered over the years. The UGRs Stock Take results (you'll learn what this means in the book), including both the quantitative results and the qualitative responses, are real outcomes from the work we did with one company. The relationship between the CEO and the senior leadership team mirrors the relationships we've seen in many an organisation. And the conversations we quote in the book are, in some cases, word-for-word replays of what we've heard when working with some of our client organisations. Of course, we've also encountered organisations with winning workplace cultures, where trust drives performance – but, by and large, this would be the exception, rather than the rule.

We believe that too many organisations are being hampered by a culture that negatively impacts on individual and collective performance. This also has a direct impact on the lives of not only the employees who are so frequently caught up in a toxic workplace culture, but also on the lives of those they hold dear. Not to mention the ripple effect that this also has on customers and suppliers. We see any workplace with a less than ideal culture as an opportunity to make the changes that will not only ensure the organisation's future success, but will make it a great place to work. Indeed, we feel that leaders owe it to themselves, their shareholders and boards, their employees, their customers and all their other stakeholders to consciously and explicitly focus on their culture - and not to leave it to chance. In fact, we believe that 'workplace culture' should be managed as a strategic objective.

It's in this context that we have written this book. We hope that it provides a grounded and practical insight into how workplace culture can be understood and changed, using the UGRs concept.

Steve and Stef
September 2015

BRUCE'S BAD DAY :

So far, even I had to admit I was not having a good vacation. I'm Bruce Bottomline—known as Mr. Fix-it to my colleagues. If you had Googled me last May 9 at 7:35 p.m., you would have learned that I was the chief operating officer of the Australian-based Very Important Corporation. And that my hairline was rapidly receding.

You could also have found a couple of flattering industry articles about me, including one that claimed, without any evidence, that I was the most optimistic senior executive in the entire Whatsit industry. You might even have found out that I earned a lot of money last year and that I had ample share options in the Very Important Corporation. Last May 9 at 7:35 p.m., you might have been forgiven for thinking that I had reasons to be cheerful.

> UGRs—Unwritten Ground Rules—are what really drive business performance. To improve organisational culture and bottom-line performance, we need to improve the UGRs.

After all, my company had, just the previous month, been ranked by *Forbes* magazine as the world's number two producer of Stuff, as the number three global organisation for Things Likely to Be

Misunderstood, and as the number one distributor of Whatsit components. The Very Important Corporation was valued at approximately $1.4 billion.

If you had seen all that when you typed my name into Google, you would have assumed that I was, like my company, on a roll.

But you would have been wrong. I was hurting. And my company was hurting. The reason for all the hurt was simple: I didn't yet understand the power of UGRs. But I didn't know that.

What hurt so bad? I could start with the uncomfortable reality that the Very Important Corporation had once been valued at over a billion dollars. On the long-awaited first day of my vacation—a vacation I had been putting off for longer than I cared to remember—our share price was valued at about ninety-eight cents and was dropping like a stone. My morale had dropped too. Right through the floor. At the time, I thought that was due to a financial problem. In fact, both our low share price and my low morale were symptoms of a culture problem. I didn't know that yet either.

> Most managers know intellectually about the importance of their culture. Paradoxically, very few understand corporate culture in bottom-line terms. Your company's culture largely determines its value.

ANNIVERSARY BLUES:

I HAD BEEN WORKING FOR THE Very Important Corporation since its founding in Sydney in August, twenty years ago. Back then, it had been a weekend project I had undertaken in the garage of my best friend, Helen W. Hardcharger, now the company's first—and only thinkable—CEO. Helen was (and is) a brilliant executive, a born overachiever. She was also the kind of person who could sell ice to an Eskimo, talk a dog off a meat wagon, and make your life miserable or wonderful, depending on what kind of day she'd decided you were supposed to have.

I suppose I should mention, too, that Helen was a bridesmaid at my wedding and that I was the best man at hers. You probably wouldn't have found out about that online, though. What you surely would have been able to piece together from your Google search was that working together for nearly thirty years, Helen and I had been the major drivers in the Very Important Corporation's long road to market dominance.

Right now, though, I wasn't thinking about work. I was thinking that it was now 7:35 p.m. on May 9, and May 10 was going to be my fifteenth wedding anniversary, no matter where I happened to be at the time. I was thinking that I was supposed to be on a nonstop flight to Honolulu to celebrate that fifteenth anniversary with my wife.

My wife was now waiting for me at a five-star beachfront hotel, and she believed I would be in our suite in time to celebrate the big day. I knew better.

TROUBLE AT THE GATE:

DON'T GET ME WRONG. I wanted desperately to be on my way to Hawaii. I had missed my flight. I had showed up at the gate at 7:35 p.m. The door had been closed firmly at 7:32 and some-odd seconds. I had pleaded in vain with the woman at the gate for some minutes before noticing my plane pulling out.

I gave up.

A grinding meeting with the Machine (our internal nickname for Helen) and the rest of our senior team had run long. I had left that meeting forty-six minutes later than I was supposed to. The belief that I might somehow still be able make my flight to Hawaii had been all that was driving me; it was the last, fleeting hope extracted from a day crammed full of insoluble crises that I inherited on that grim, endlessly depressing day May 9.

Now, normally, I really am an optimistic, upbeat person, the kind of guy who can fix just about any problem with a smile on his face, the kind of guy who instinctively sees the glass as half full. That's why everyone calls me Mr. Fix-it.

I always protest the nickname, but the truth is, I secretly like it. On a good day, I feel like Mr. Fix-it.

But May 9 was not a good day. As I pondered the grim, flickering text on the departures screen in the crowded airport lobby,

I didn't feel at all like Mr. Fix-it. I was not feeling particularly optimistic by any stretch of the imagination.

I was, in fact, seriously considering leaving the Very Important Corporation for good.

This wasn't just because I had missed my flight out of Sydney and, as a result, missed my own anniversary.

I had been considering quitting long before my absurd problems at check-in. For reasons known only to her, a squat security employee felt I represented an unresolved problem of some kind and made me go through two separate security screenings. (Maybe my facial expression matched something she had been trained to notice about people who are eager to blow things up.)

> Long-term, unaddressed cultural problems can lead to the loss of key people, and other problems.

The long wait in line had given me time to think about my day, which was the very last thing I wanted to do.

May 9 at the Very Important Corporation had been the kind of experience that curdled one's lemonade into a sour, undrinkable heated-Jell-O mass of yellow toxic goop. My day (as I had confided to my personal assistant, Sally, just before leaving for the airport) had sucked.

SALLY IS SHOCKED

BACK AT THE OFFICE, SALLY'S eyes had widened when I'd said that word to her. Sally had been worried about me for a while, but this word made her gasp.

Sally knew that words like "sucked" had never before, in her very good memory, escaped the lips of Mr. Fix-it, for whom she had worked loyally since 1997. My highest rhetorical pitch when frustrated had, up to that point, been the words "Good gravy." And I'd saved that expression for very special occasions.

After Sally had heard me complain that my day had sucked, she had seen me out the door of my office, looking relieved that I was finally going to get some time off. I had been working a steady succession of eighteen-hour days for the past five weeks.

And for the record, I was 100 percent right about last May 9. It had sucked.

As the day began, I knew that the Very Important Corporation's quarterly earnings were about to be announced, and when they were, I knew that shareholders were not going to like what they heard one little bit.

What was even more troubling was the news that Milt Smooth, our company's VP of sales, had that afternoon been admitted to the hospital with heart trouble. Milt had been with the company for fourteen years. He had started out as a field salesperson. I had hired him. Milt was only forty-seven; he had a wife and four kids. Milt was now in the intensive care unit.

MILT'S LITTLE SECRET V:

MILT'S SUDDEN HOSPITALISATION HAD FOLLOWED a meeting with Helen, which had followed the unwelcome news, received that very morning, that our company's single biggest customer, the energy giant Drillco, had cancelled all its yearly orders of Stuff and Whatsit. This cancellation represented a $400 million blow to cash flow, and it also meant that next quarter's earnings report was going to look even worse than this one's.

So far, fewer than a dozen people knew about this order cancellation. I was one. Milt was another. Helen Hardcharger was another.

More people were eventually going to find out, though. And it seemed quite likely that they were about to find out imminently because someone at Drillco had been leaking unflattering information about the Very Important Corporation to industry magazines and websites for nearly a year.

VI:
EXIT THE AMERICAN?

DRILLCO'S PRESIDENT HAD CANCELLED THE orders only with great reluctance and after persistent delays in both production and delivery. These delays had plagued our company for nearly twelve months.

As vice president of operations, I was ultimately responsible for fixing these problems. I had tried to fix them. I had failed.

As though all of that hadn't been enough for one day, I had, on May 9, heard from a highly reliable source (namely my assistant, Sally) that the "word on the street" was that our company's hotshot young consultant, "the American", Dave Dude, had all but made up his mind to exercise his option to leave us. He would, the rumour had it, be starting his own consulting firm. This was deep inside stuff, a devastating but untraceable rumour that no one had been able to confirm or deny, and thus commanded the highest level of credibility within our organisation.

After two years working in the same building with her, Dave hated Helen Hardcharger, and everyone knew it. Including Helen.

On May 9, I became aware, at about the same time as Helen, that there was no longer any plausible reason to believe that Dave would not jump ship and take our most important clients with him.

This was bad news. When "the American" had come on board, he had negotiated a tough contract—because we had been so eager to get him to sign quickly. The contract gave Dave considerable leeway when it came to determining what did and didn't constitute direct competition. According to Sally, Dave had had his attorneys review it closely for over a week.

> Cliques, feuds, and rivalries are a sign that your organisation's UGRs aren't supporting your team.

The news of Dave's apparently imminent departure, and the inevitable loss of some of our most important clients, would send the Very Important Corporation's share price plummeting even further when it became public (which it inevitably would).

Truly, May 9 had indeed sucked. And missed flight or no missed flight, May 10 could not come fast enough for me.

VII

DAVE GETS A WARNING

THE RIFT WITH DAVE DUDE was not exactly a new development. Dave had clashed publicly with Helen Hardcharger during a high-profile all-company meeting about a month and a half after signing on with us, and things had gone downhill from there.

That all-company meeting had followed a wave of team-building events centred around our company's stated "core values": communication, respect, integrity, and excellence. In an effort to "live" those values, our people had climbed rock walls, hurled themselves at great speed along zip lines, and caught each other while falling backward, blindfolded.

No one had actually died during any of these team-building events, which I personally considered a major organisational accomplishment. But there were a few folks who told me afterward they wished they had. Dave Dude was one of those people.

But I'm getting ahead of myself. As the team-building event began, Dave Dude, the natural brainstormer and brilliant tactician we had just lured away from our biggest competitor, did not yet hate Helen Hardcharger. To the contrary, Dave had caught the spirit of the event full-on. Flush with excitement, he had shared what he thought were some creative ideas in response to Helen's challenge to the group to "take our company to the next level."

During one of the scheduled brainstorming sessions, Dave had started free-associating. He was talking a mile a minute, getting the whole team pumped, which was, truth be told, a big part of the reason we had hired him away from the competition. We wanted him to free-associate. We wanted him to talk a mile a minute. We wanted him to get the rest of the company pumped. And we wanted new ideas.

Among Dave's innovative ideas that afternoon was one about changing the executive compensation plan at the Very Important Corporation.

Over two years later, standing in the airport reticketing line, I could still hear the icy silence that had followed Dave's breathless attempt to live up to the themes of communication, respect, integrity, and excellence that we had been talking about all weekend. I could still see lanky Helen Hardcharger staring down the diminutive Dave Dude. And I could still hear Helen Hardcharger break the agonisingly long gap with these words: "Be careful, young man."

I wasn't sure why I found myself thinking of that awful moment now, as I waited in line to get a new ticket to Honolulu. I had other things to worry about. Like what I would say to my wife when I finally called to tell her I would be arriving a day late for our anniversary. And whether it really was, at long last, time for me to move on and leave the Very Important Corporation.

> A single toxic comment from a senior leader can undo weeks, months, or even years of team building.

VIII: ENTER THE WEIRDO

"**W**ELCOME."

The guy sitting next to me in first class—a genial elderly man wearing a pair of ridiculously out-of-style Benjamin Franklin glasses—apparently wanted to talk. I suppressed a sigh of disgust. Talk was the last thing I wanted. This day, I concluded, really would never end.

"Around here," he said, "we think positive and look for solutions. Am I right?"

It might not have been the strangest thing I'd heard all day, but it was pretty close.

"Around here," he repeated, "we think positive and look for solutions. Is that a deal?"

"Okay," I said. It came out sounding a lot more serious than I'd meant it.

"Good," he said. "Good."

I stared out the window, as though the midnight tarmac held some deep secret it was my responsibility to unearth. I was hoping against hope that my new "friend" would get the message and shut up. I wasn't in the market for a red-eye travel buddy with a penchant for motivational clichés. If the old fellow,

14

who looked about eighty, really needed someone to keep him company on the long flight to Honolulu, he could switch seats easily enough.

I must have been muttering to myself, and more tired than I thought, because the white-haired man said pleasantly, "But I don't want to switch seats."

My mouth suddenly went dry. The runway glistened with red and white runway lights. The PA system announced that we were ready for takeoff.

Was I that far gone? Had the day been that bad?

Well, yes. Surely, I must have been; how else would he—

"So—how did she take the news, Bruce?"

I turned and stared at the old man.

"How did who," I asked carefully, "take what news?"

He smiled. "Your wife," he said patiently, "how did she take the news that you would not be seeing her until the day after your anniversary?"

My mind raced through the various unlikely possibilities. A gag that Helen might somehow have set up? A cable comedy show, say, based on videotaping the victims of practical jokes? But I had just gotten the new tickets. How could anyone have known the new itinerary? Maybe some kind of cyber-stalker? Some new form of corporate espionage?

The old man chuckled.

"Don't look so alarmed. I've done a lot of research on you, that's all," he promised. "And no, you're not going to be getting a divorce. Your wife, Muriel, just forgave you on Facebook. Sally posted a note telling her she didn't think you were going to make your flight. Sally's my niece, you know. You and I are practically family."

Silence.

The flight attendant? Nowhere in sight. Push the call button?

"Relax." The old man smiled. "She confides in me. We're about to take off."

The great jet's engines gunned. We began to grind forward.

IX: WHO AUTHORIZED THIS?

"**O**KAY," I SAID, DARING AUDIBLE words at last. "Did Sally ask you to follow me?"

The cabin darkened. The white-haired man leaned toward me and whispered purposefully, "That's one way to look at it. Personally, I prefer to believe she asked me to keep an eye on you."

"Why?"

"Because you need me."

I took a deep breath.

"I sure as hell need something," I said, nursing the Scotch that the auburn-haired flight attendant had proffered just before telling me to buckle my seat belt.

"So, I assume you heard all about today," I said, grim.

"I certainly did," he replied.

"Great," I grumbled.

"I do have a question for you."

"What's that?"

"Bruce," the old man said, "I want you to tell me whether you really do believe, deep down in your heart..."

"What? Believe what?"

"That communication, respect, integrity, and excellence are the values your company is living by—right now, today."

Somehow, his eyes shone through the dim half-light of the cabin. They were blue and piercing and seemed astonishingly alert for a man of his age.

Without waiting for my answer, the plane grabbed the night sky and took off.

X
SAM'S NUMBER ONE PROJECT:

"**I**T'S AN EXTREMELY IMPORTANT QUESTION, Bruce. Believe me, you want to answer it. Now, let me share something important at this particular juncture. I have nothing to gain here, so you can tell me everything." The old fellow spoke that last sentence soothingly, then handed me a business card. It read:

Sam Sherlock
Culture-by-Design Consultant (Ret.)
Brooklyn, New York

Apparently, Sally had American relatives. Strange ones, at that. I was afraid to ask him what he was doing in Sydney.

"You are my number one project, Bruce, though I want you to know that I do only pro bono work now. I will never charge you a single dollar for my time. With a little help from Sally – all above board of course - I have been working on your company for months. You should know that, at this stage of my career, I seek out only the clients I like. Funny thing. The clients who need me most usually don't *know* they need me. That's where you are right now."

I shifted in my seat and tried not to look at him.

"By the way," he said reassuringly, "the entirety of our conversation tonight is confidential. What you say to me stays with me. Sally doesn't get to hear a word of it, and neither does anyone else. I take it to my grave. That is my promise, Bruce, and I never! Ever! Ever! Go back on a promise." He wagged a bony finger in my face three times, once for each exclamation point, paused for a moment to make sure I had not lost count, then put the finger away.

"Now, all day long," he continued, "you've been dealing with two things you don't need: bad news and double-talk. Here we are, on our way to Hawaii at last, and you've finally got the ear of someone who's going to give you nothing but straight talk—assuming, of course, that you tell me the truth. That is a promise, too, Bruce. And please remember that I never! Ever! Ever! Go back on a—"

"I've got it," I said. "You don't break your promises. You can put your finger down now."

He did.

"You will want to take full advantage of this particular consultation, I can assure you of that, Bruce. And let me tell you something else. Sally's got an instinct for when people are about to leave, and she thinks you're headed for the door. If Helen knew you were about to quit, she'd want you to take full advantage of this consultation, too. I can guarantee you that. So, let's be frank with each other, because you have nothing to lose. You are about to leave the company, are you not?"

I looked away.

"Of course not."

He tsk-tsked, apparently disappointed.

"Bruce, Bruce, Bruce." My name sounded like the saddest word in the world coming out of his mouth. "We've already covered this part. I can't possibly help you, or the company, if you don't tell me the truth. You've put the best part of your life into this company, haven't you?"

I thought for a moment, then heard myself say, "Yes. I am about to quit."

"Which brings me back to my first question. Do you really believe, deep down in your heart, that communication, respect, integrity, and excellence are the values your company is living by—right now, today?"

I pondered this for a long moment, then said, "No. No, of course not."

"Excellent!" he said, grinning broadly. "Of course you're not. That's your first piece of good news today. You told the truth. You and I now know for sure that that's not really the kind of company you work for. Now, tell me please: Why *aren't* people living by those values at your company?"

I considered this and then actually told the truth, the whole truth, and nothing but the truth to a little grey man who, just a few minutes earlier, had been a total stranger: "Because Helen and the senior team don't actually live by those values."

"Marvellous!" the little man shouted, loud enough that I feared he would draw the attention of the stewardess. "The second piece of good news of the day. Now we're really getting somewhere, Bruce. By the way, those words you've got your people reciting all day long, those words you're plastering all over the place and building all your press releases around, would you mind saying them out loud one more time for me?"

"No, I don't mind at all," I said. "Communication, respect, integrity, and excellence."

"Do you know who else said they had those values?"

"No," I said. "Who?"

"Enron," he whispered, his bony hand concealing the word from the rest of the passengers. I knew all too well that Enron was once the seventh-largest US company; it was now legendary as that country's largest corporate collapse.

Suddenly, I felt even more ill than I had before. If this guy was here on Sally's behalf to help me feel better, she needed to know he was doing a lousy job.

XI
AN E-MAIL EXCHANGE
XI:

"**D**O YOU MIND MY ASKING," Sam said as he poured some spring water into a glass, "where those four words came from? Whose idea they were?"

He took a long sip and watched me carefully.

"They weren't from you, I take it."

"No. Helen just announced them via e-mail late one night. It was years ago. Said we all had to follow them. You'd have to know her, I guess. That's just the kind of leader she is. She said that these four values reflected the kind of company she wanted to build. She told us all that these were the values we were going to follow. Period. End of discussion."

"Mm-hmm. And just out of curiosity, how did she decide that those values, out of all the possible values she could have chosen, were the right ones for you and your company to focus on?"

This question brought back an old, old argument, conducted via e-mail, between me and Helen. I still remembered the exchange verbatim.

To: Helen
Fr: Bruce

RE: "Communication, respect, integrity, and excellence."

Can I ask where we picked these values up, and why we chose them?

Shouldn't I get a look at this kind of thing, and perhaps a word or two of feedback, before you CC everyone in the company?

To: Bruce
Fr: Helen

RE: "Communication, respect, integrity, and excellence."

Saw them in Forbes. I liked them as values. They're where we're going.

If you think I'm going to run everything by you for approval, you're out of your freaking mind.

Get on board.

To: Helen
Fr: Bruce

RE: "Communication, respect, integrity, and excellence."

So much for communication and respect. I'll keep an eye out for integrity and excellence.

Taking some time off.

I realised Sam was still waiting for me to speak.

"They came from Helen," I admitted. "Why she chose those values specifically, I couldn't tell you. I suspect she simply liked the way they looked on a memo."

"The truth is, Bruce," Sam said, "those words that you guys put up on your posters really don't mean much of *anything* because they're not the actual ground rules that guide your organisation."

He paused for a moment to let that one sink in. Then he said, "In the real world, you and your people live by a very different set of ground rules. Am I right?"

Who the hell was this guy?

"Well, am I? Either I am right or I'm not."

He was. But I had never actually said so out loud.

"Yes," I said. "You are right. The rules we really live by are quite different. But if this is a lecture about organisational culture, I'm afraid I'm not up for it tonight, and anyway, that's a complicated topic that takes years to address. I'm not just talking about our company. It's

> Words that you put up on your bulletin board or paste into your annual report don't mean anything if they don't reflect the actual Unwritten Ground Rules your company lives by.

> Identifying the actual culture your company lives by is easier than you think.

any company. It's hard to change these things, probably impossible. I think even identifying the actual culture that a company lives by is a very, very difficult thing to do."

"No, it's not," said Sam Sherlock.

XII.

HELEN, MOVING ON

HELEN HARDCHARGER WAS NOT EASILY distracted.

Her company's share price was plunging. One of her senior executives was in the hospital. Another was leaving, almost certainly to start a marketplace rival. And a third (me, although Helen didn't know it yet) was getting ready to leave the company and end a friendship of three decades' standing. Helen Hardcharger, however, was, as always, moving on.

"Donna!"

She was calling Donna Messwidme, her tough-as-nails executive assistant. Donna had been working for Helen for eleven years and knew her better than anyone in the company—excepting, perhaps, me.

"Yes, Helen?"

She had somehow materialised at the door of her office the second before Helen had barked her name. She did this twelve to fifteen times a day; it was one of her most remarkable skills. Drawing and maintaining boundaries with Helen was another. No one was quite sure how she pulled off either feat.

"Our customer satisfaction scores are going down the toilet. I want you to get Bruce to do something about it."

A tenth of a second passed. To an outsider, it would hardly have seemed a pause at all, but between Helen and Donna, it was an eternity.

Helen shot her a deadly glance.

"Bruce is on a short vacation for his anniversary, Helen. Sally says he seems to be going through a rough patch."

"That's too goddamned bad. I don't care what kind of patch he's going through. I want you to get me voice to voice with him the minute you can. Tell him I have had a breakthrough. These customer satisfaction scores are our real problem. They're what's dragging the whole organisation down. What they're telling me is that our frontline people—hell, all our people—just are not treating our customers with respect. Respect is our middle name, for God's sake! Now listen. I want you to forward these scores to Bruce and tell him that I need this fixed. Now. Any employee, anywhere in the organisation, who disrespects a customer is going to see his name and face up on the Wall of Shame after the first occurrence, is going to get disciplinary action after the second occurrence, and is going to be fired after the third occurrence. Three strikes, and you're out! Set up the call, Donna."

Donna thought, for the tiniest fraction of a second, of telling Helen, "You want me to interrupt a man's fifteenth wedding anniversary to tell him that we are all about respect?"

What Donna actually said, being careful not to show the tiniest shred of irony or frustration in her tone, was, "Okay, Helen."

Donna and all the others in the company knew that Helen was never, ever to be told she was mistaken.

This insight had profound implications on, among other things, our share price. As yet, no one, and certainly not Helen, had identified that as a problem.

VIII

SO CLOSE, BUT YET SO FAR

XIII:

I DID NOT KNOW ABOUT ANY of that, of course. I was still on a flight to Hawaii, sitting next to Sam Sherlock, exhausted and trying my level best to tell him the truth, because ignoring him simply didn't work.

I had just told him what I honestly believed to be the case: that it was a difficult business, identifying any organisation's working culture.

And Sam had just told me I was wrong.

"It's actually pretty easy to identify a company's working culture, Bruce," he said calmly. "Despite anything to the contrary that people may have told you about this, despite anything insiders, consultants, and other self-appointed experts may have predicted about what your organisation's internal problems are or aren't, despite anything you may have read, the concept of organisational culture is *not* difficult to understand. People think it's difficult to understand, usually because they don't really know what culture is."

> Organisational culture is the collection of Unwritten Ground Rules, or UGRs, that drive people's behaviour in the workplace.

"Okay," I said. "I'll bite. What is organisational culture?"

"Organisational culture," Sam answered, "is simply people's perceptions of 'the way we do things around here.' It's the collection of 'Unwritten Ground Rules,' or UGRs, that drive people's behaviours in the workplace."

"Notice," Sam continued, "that the UGRs are not necessarily based on what we *want* people's perceptions to be about a certain issue. It's what the perceptions *actually are* in any given area. It's the way our people would finish the sentence 'Around here,...' if they felt comfortable enough with us to share the truth about what they really felt."

> UGRs reflect people's actual (and typically unspoken) perceptions of "the way we do things around here."

Sam watched me closely with the slightest trace of a smile on his face, as though he were curious to learn whether I had grasped the importance of what he had just shared with me.

"UGRs are the *real* culture, Bruce. Think about what it's like starting a new job. UGRs are the culture you have to pick up, and learn to operate within, during your first few weeks on the job if you want to avoid getting in trouble or getting fired. Of course, it's not always what goes into the manual. In fact, it may not be written down anywhere. But culture is much more powerful than any rules that could be written down, because it's what people actually do. It's what shapes perceptions, relationships, and actions in the real world.

> UGRs shape perceptions, relationships, and actions in the workplace.

"So," Sam went on, "how are UGRs created and sustained? Not by writing an e-mail about communication, respect, and integrity, hitting 'send,' and then crossing 'culture' off your to-do list.

In the workplace, there are three major ways UGRs are shaped. The first way is, *people watch what gets noticed."*

"For instance, if someone gets into trouble for speaking up, then one UGR might be 'Around here, you'd better not say what's really on your mind, even if you're asked directly for your opinion by someone in authority.' A single incident, very often, creates or solidifies an organisation's UGRs."

> The first way in which UGRs are created: people watch what gets noticed. This creates and shapes the UGRs within any company or team.

The moment I heard Sam say this, my mind raced back to the fateful moment of Helen's pointed exchange with Dave Dude during our company-wide meeting. For a brief instant, I literally felt physically ill as I thought of how close we had seemed to be to changing the way we did things at the Very Important Corporation. We had, I now sensed, been close, powerfully close, to creating the kind of environment in which people could and did speak their minds when they thought doing so would help the company. And then Helen had said, "Be careful, young man."

Before that awful scene, I had thought we were turning the corner as an organisation.

XIV.
HELEN THE DESTROYER

WE HAD JUST SPENT TWO days coming together as a team. I had been preparing the organisation for that critical all-employee team-building event for at least three months, manoeuvring every public and private diplomatic lever available to me. Specifically, I had pleaded with Helen to hold her tongue when tempted to criticise, verbally attack, or humiliate someone, and let me fix whatever the problem was and employ my considerable personal charm on behalf of our supposed "values"

A single memorable incident can create or solidify a UGR. This principle can operate for the betterment of an organisation, or it can make things worse.

of communication, respect, integrity, and excellence. I had gotten six hundred people in the same room at the same time to buy into the proposition that Helen Hardcharger in her worst moments was not what the company was all about. And I was ecstatic. And wonder of wonders, it was working. We had all shared forty-eight straight hours of constructive, forward-thinking, positive collaborative action. We had eaten meals together. We had overcome physical and emotional challenges together. We had created and implemented solutions together.

And then Helen had destroyed it all.

She had done so by grabbing that microphone and issuing that horrible threat: "Be careful, young man."

Not "We'll talk about this later." Not "Interesting idea." But "Be careful, young man." The ghastly silence that followed that sentence still made my heart race and my fists clench in a way that was, I knew, part of the problem and not part of the solution. In fact, I had purposefully avoided thinking of this moment for a very specific reason: thinking of it always made me want to quit my job. And I found I wanted to quit now more than ever.

SOME NASTY RULES

XV:

IT OCCURRED TO ME THAT Sam had been silently regarding me for some time as I thought through all this.

"By the same token," Sam went on, breaking the tactful pause as though my little mental cramp had not taken place at all, "people watch what doesn't get noticed. For instance, if someone speaks badly of a manager, and nobody suggests that people shouldn't talk that way, then a UGR might be 'Around here, it's fine to criticise bosses, as long as you do it behind their backs.' So, that's the second way UGRs get created and reinforced: people notice what doesn't get noticed."

> The second way in which UGRs are created: people watch what doesn't get noticed.

I thought of all the toxic water cooler talk that I had listened to over the years at the Very Important Corporation and how I had simply listened in. I thought of the dramatic way a group's tone of voice changed whenever a senior executive came near and of the countless conversations I had accidentally overheard in which people had aired their various grievances against Helen or other senior people. I'd even heard myself described as "Helen's errand boy" by one unhappy staff member who had no idea I was in the next room.

"Of course, what *doesn't* end up getting noticed by other people could also affect the company. For instance, if a person goes out of her way to help a colleague, but her boss never recognises that extra effort, then one UGR might be 'Around here, it's not worth your while to help others out.'"

He looked and sounded nothing like me, but I realised that listening to Sam talk about all this was like listening to a better, wiser version of myself. I thought of how hard it was at our company to get people to pitch in on projects that didn't have their own name printed on the front page. I also thought of the relentless daily habit that drove most of the employees at our organisation, pursued as though it were a religious obligation—the habit of heading out the door at five o'clock on the dot. I knew there were companies that didn't operate like this. I had seen and envied many such workplaces. But I had always believed that the reason they operated differently than we did had something to do with the talent level of the individuals that they'd hired. Now I was beginning to see that I could take the very same people, put them in our organisation, ignore them or fail to acknowledge them appropriately, and very quickly indeed either drive them to quit or bring them around to our way of thinking: *Around here, it's not worth your while to help others out.*

And with the job market as brutally competitive as it was, could I really say that I was all that surprised when good people, talented people, well-intentioned people, chose to stay in their cubicles and follow this UGR, just like everyone around them was doing?

> People "read" what does and doesn't get noticed by management more carefully than they read any human resource manual. What we read in the responses of managers creates and shapes the UGRs within any company or team.

"In addition," Sam said, "people watch closely for differences between what people say and what they do, especially differences between what *managers* say and what *managers* do. If a manager says, 'In this organisation, we respect and care for our people,' and soon after that, the same person treats a person without respect, then a UGR might be 'Around here, the bosses say one thing and mean another.' That gives us the third way teams and organisations create UGRs: managers either act in harmony with what they say or they don't."

The painful conclusions Sam had just outlined, I realised, really were our UGRs at the Very Important Corporation. They really were "the way we did things around here." As Sam sipped his ice water, I rolled them over in my mind:

The third way in which UGRs are created: people watch to see whether what managers say matches up with what they do. This too creates UGRs.

- *Around here, you'd better not say what's really on your mind, even if you're asked directly for your opinion by someone in authority.*
- *Around here, it's fine to criticise the bosses, as long as you do it behind their backs.*
- *Around here, it's not worth your while to help others out.*
- *Around here, the bosses say one thing but mean another.*

Even as I heard myself say them out loud, I knew instinctively that this probably wasn't a comprehensive list of all the UGRs by which we operated, but it was nevertheless an astonishingly accurate picture of what was driving the behaviour in our workplace day after day. And it was also, I knew (without quite being able to say why), the reason that we were in trouble.

XVI:

"**S** O? HOW CLOSE AM I?" Sam asked.

"Bull's-eye. That's us," I said to Sam, astonished. "You've described our actual operating principles, or at least some of them. I don't know how you did it, but you nailed them. That's the way we really do things at our company right now. We're doomed."

"Easy there," he said. "We think positive and look for solutions, right?"

In spite of myself, I laughed.

Sam smiled. "So anyway. You're sure it's not communication, respect, integrity, and excellence that are driving the Very Important Corporation right now?"

"Pretty sure," I said. "Listen, Sam," I continued. "I have to ask you a question. Are these the only UGRs that are dragging our company down, do you think? Or are there others?"

"There are plenty of others." He winked at me. "Bet on it."

"So, how the hell do we figure out how many of these UGRs exist, what they're really telling people, and which need fixing first?"

"You want the short answer first or the long answer?" Sam asked.

"Let's try the short answer," I said hopefully.

"No, these aren't the only UGRs you have to worry about. Yes, there are others you will need to identify. And in order to spot them and eventually change them to something better, someone who cares deeply about both the people and the business is going to have to find a way to get the entire management team on board. And the key word here is 'entire.'"

I didn't much like the sound of all that.

"By 'someone,' am I to understand that you mean me?"

In answer, Sam only signalled the flight attendant for a new bottle of spring water. Once that had been provided, he winked at me once again, as though he had granted me admittance to some kind of secret club.

XVII

XVII: DEAL OF THE CENTURY

"**T**HE MAIN THING TO REMEMBER about UGRs," Sam went on cheerfully, as though I had already agreed to be his accomplice, "is that they are *unwritten*. Often unspoken too. That means they are rarely, or never, documented or included in policy manuals, training sessions, or anything else that leaves a paper trail. In fact, UGRs often run exactly opposite to what appears in the policy manuals, mission statements, and orientation programs of the organisation. Some UGRs from companies I've worked with would probably sound very familiar to you. Others would be unique to a certain work environment."

> UGRs often run counter to formal mission statements, on-boarding programs, and policies. This fact often increases disaffection in the workforce, based on a feeling that management does not "walk its talk."

"So how did we find them?" I asked.

"Easy. I can walk you through the process via conference calls and make sure you dot all the i's and cross all the t's. And I won't charge you a thing. But there's a catch."

"What's that?"

"It's a long-standing policy of mine. You only get this particular service free of charge *if...*"

"If what?"

"*If* you happen to be the only guy in the whole organisation who's got a chance in hell of getting the CEO to change her ways. Everybody else," Sam Sherlock whispered, "pays full price. What a deal, eh?"

XVIII: IMA

A T THAT VERY MOMENT, THE most recently hired employee at the Very Important Corporation was a tough young research assistant named Ima Starr.

Ima stood four foot eleven in stocking feet, but woe to the person who mistook her small stature for vulnerability. Ima was not to be trifled with in an interoffice squabble. She prided herself on her street smarts, and she had just figured out how things really worked at our company. She had accomplished this in just three days.

Like so many new employees, Ima was like a busy little sponge, absorbing all the information she possibly could about the way things really worked at the Very Important Corporation. Without knowing anything about the concept of UGRs, Ima had picked up many of the cultural driving forces within the company, including:

- *Around here, the only time you get called into a private meeting with Helen is either when you do something wrong or she wants something.*

- *Around here, Helen talks about respect. But we all know she doesn't really mean it. So we don't really have to do anything.*
- *Around here, we go through the motions with our bosses, but once they're gone, you can do pretty much what you want.*
- *Around here, there is no use complaining about anything at meetings, because nothing ever gets done.*
- *Around here, the best jokes are the ones you make at the expense of a supervisor or co-worker who is not around.*

New employees learn an organisation's UGRs—whether those UGRs support the bottom line or detract from it—with startling speed. This is one reason that UGRs have such remarkable power within the organisations they guide. They are perceived as essential survival tactics, typically from the very earliest days of one's involvement with the team.

After only three days, Ima was now well positioned to climb the ladder of success at the Very Important Corporation. The only problem was, at the rate we were going, there was likely to be no ladder to climb and no company at which to climb it.

XIX: THE VALUES THING

"**L**ET ME GET JUST A little more help from you on the whole 'communication, respect, integrity, and excellence' thing," I said to Sam as casually as I could.

"Yes?"

"How do we know," I said, "that those *aren't* really the values we should be shooting for? I mean, I know Helen basically picked them out of a hat. But that doesn't make them wrong. Or does it? Is the problem that we didn't pick the right values? Or is there some other reason we're having so much trouble following through on them?"

Sam put his water down and leaned forward a little bit so he could make eye contact with more than his usual twinkle power.

"I'll tell you a little secret, Bruce. I really don't like talking about values very much. My wife always says that values are something people get at discount stores.

"She exaggerates, of course, but you get her point. People and organisations get side-tracked by all this talk about values. Usually, 'values' don't have anything at all to do with what's actually happening in your company. They don't usually connect

43

to actions and agreements. Right now, what you need to focus on identifying are not the right values, whatever those are, but the right key cultural attributes, or KCAs."

"What's the difference between values and KCAs?"

"Values," Sam explained, "are the principles that outline how people relate and behave. They are the broad rules of the game, the parameters within which the game is expected to be played. An organisation's values at any given moment may or may not be what people say they are. The folks at Enron said that one of their guiding values was integrity. Looking at how things played out for them, I'm not so sure that was actually part of the rules they played the game by."

"Me neither," I admitted.

"KCAs, on the other hand, are the cultural tactics that are necessary for the game to be won. They're what you do within your culture to achieve your goal within the team context to heighten the chances of your strategic goals being realised. So, the question we really need to look at, Bruce, is what are the current tactics operating within your culture, and how good a job are they doing of getting you closer to achieving your goals? And what key cultural attributes are necessary for this company to be truly successful?"

"That's a pretty big question," I said, admiring Sam's impeccable clarity.

> "KCAs" stands for "key cultural attributes." KCAs are those aspects of the culture that need to be in place for the organisation to succeed in the future. For example, "quality interdepartmental relationships" is an example of a key cultural attribute.

"It is indeed," he replied, smiling. "It's a *huge* question for any company, for any organisation, big or small, for profit or not-for-profit. The trouble is, Bruce, most companies don't bother to ask it."

Values are the broad cultural rules of the game; for instance, "respect" is an example of a value. They are notoriously hard to quantify. People of good intent can have very different, or completely contradictory, understandings of what a given value means.

XX: HELEN'S NASTY TEXT

HELEN HARDCHARGER SENT HER SECRETARY a profane text message demanding to know when I would be checking in to discuss her latest ideas about improving attitudes toward customers at the Very Important Corporation. It read (more or less), "When the bleep is Bruce getting off his bleeping plane so I can bleeping talk to him about the respect initiative, exclamation point, exclamation point, exclamation point."

This text showed up shortly after 11:00 p.m. Donna, her assistant, pretended not to see it.

XXI: THE FIVE MONKEYS

SAM TORE THE YELLOW SHEET from his legal pad where he'd been making brief notes, scanned its densely inscribed surface one last time, then folded it briskly into a precise rectangle. He then produced a crisp white envelope from his coat pocket. Astonishingly, the envelope bore my name in Sam's careful, textbook-perfect handwriting. He inserted the yellow sheet in the envelope, then flipped the envelope over, gave it three short licks, and sealed it. He handed it to me.

"So shall we give this a try? You agree to check in with me by phone regularly?" He stared at me expectantly.

I took the envelope. But what on earth was I agreeing to?

"Purely theoretically, mind you," I said to Sam, "if I were to agree to make these calls with you, I would need the answers to a few questions."

"Such as?"

"Well, for instance—what would happen if Helen simply left the company? Would the negative UGRs go with her?"

"Probably not," Sam said, "unless somebody who really cared about the organisation did the work necessary to replace them with positive ones, and then taught people how to support those positive UGRs over time. Without that effort, a fair number of the negative UGRs would likely stay in place for years, or even decades."

"For decades? Are you serious?"

"Let me tell you a story," Sam said. And here's what he told me.

The Tale of Five Monkeys

Years ago, a group of white-coated scientists gathered five monkeys and placed them in a large cage. In the cage was a ladder, and dangling enticingly above the ladder was a bunch of bananas. In terms of its construction, the cage was completely identical to any number of other cages that might have contained the monkeys except for one fascinating feature. It had sprinklers built into the ceiling.

Not long after the scientists placed them in the cage, the monkeys spotted the bananas. They began their climb up the ladder and the minute they did, the scientists pressed a switch that turned on the sprinklers. The poor monkeys got drenched.

The monkeys kept looking longingly at the bananas, though, and of course, they tried again. But the same thing happened to them on their second attempt up the ladder. The sprinklers were switched on, and they got soaked through.

This happened again and again. Eventually, the monkeys gave up trying to get the bananas.

The scientists then removed one of the monkeys and put a new monkey into the cage. The new one spotted the bananas and, naturally, made his way over to climb the ladder. That was when something extraordinary happened.

Before the new monkey even made it to the second rung of the ladder, the other monkeys attacked him. They jumped on him aggressively from all directions and did everything they could to pull the new monkey off the ladder. And they succeeded.

The new monkey tried again a few minutes later and once again he found himself assaulted before he could make an ascent toward the bananas.

Again, and again he tried, but each time, the new monkey faced the same consequence: physical assault. Eventually the new monkey, too, ceased trying.

The scientists then took another one of the original monkeys out and replaced it with a new one. You can predict what happened. The new monkey tried to climb the ladder and was set upon, repeatedly, by his companions - including the recently arrived replacement - until he stopped trying to climb the ladder.

The scientists repeated this process until it had a group composed entirely of new monkeys. All the original monkeys who had been sprayed with the sprinkler had been removed from the cage. Only new monkeys remained.

The scientists then placed another new monkey in the cage. When he made a move for the bananas, the other monkeys instantly pulled him down to the ground.

Why?

Not one of them had a clue.

XVII XXII:

THE TO-DO LIST DESCENDS TO A SINGLE IMPORTANT ITEM

I SIPPED WHAT WAS LEFT OF a glass of red wine and stared out at the bright, cold, and cloudless dawn rising over the Pacific Ocean.

"So, what am I supposed to do now?" I asked. "Fly blind? Wave this piece of paper you've written out for me in front of everyone and wait for all the problems in my company to disappear?"

"Whose company did you say this was, Bruce?" Sam was smiling.

I grunted and avoided the question. "Even if it does feel like something I've built, even if it is something that's part of me, the truth is, this company has also become something that's killing me. I'm not giving myself a heart attack for Helen Hardcharger. I've had enough."

> To improve the culture using UGRs requires close consideration of a five-step process.

"Now, that's the smartest thing I've heard you say this whole trip." Sam beamed. "You've reached the threshold point. Now all that's left for you to do is decide which of the two roads in front of you are worth walking. Are you going to go your own way or are you going to fix what's broken?"

The long shadow in the cabin vanished as the overhead lights clicked on. A voice above them said, "We are now making our final descent, and we will be landing in Honolulu in approximately thirty minutes. Please fasten your seat belts in preparation for landing."

I took my last swig of red wine and breathed deeply.

"All right," I said, "I will try this. I will follow your little checklist and check in with you by phone on one condition. She's going to have to accept some accountability. If she won't take some of the responsibility here, if she won't hear me out and agree to make some major changes in the way she operates, with me and everyone else, if she won't let me be the one to decide whether she has changed, then I'm walking out the door."

"Excellent. And in the event you don't decide to walk out the door, you and I will work through the five-step UGRs process, which we can use to improve the culture."

Prior to moving on to the five steps for cultural change, prior to even talking about them with anyone in your organisation, there has to be total support for constructive change from the senior leadership team and total accountability from that team.

"Before you do anything, though, you need an agreement. You need to have your little heart-to-heart with Helen. Everything you were just saying about her—figuring out that accountability begins at home, that it's time for a change, that there will be major consequences if there is no change—that all has to come first. Prior to moving on to the five steps, prior to even talking about them, there has to be total support for constructive change from the senior leadership team. You haven't got that yet, and until you do, it would be a waste of time and energy to move on to the five steps that can build new UGRs for you."

"So what do I do right now?"

"That's simple," Sam answered, tightening his seat belt. "You go on vacation."

That seemed like a great place to start the project, so I took Sam's advice. For two straight weeks, I enjoyed Hawaii with my wife and did not speak to, text, or even think all that much about anyone at the Very Important Corporation. I had more important things to do.

XVIII XXIII:

HELEN'S INIMITABLE PEOPLE SKILLS ON DISPLAY ONCE AGAIN

"WHAT THE HELL WERE YOU thinking?" Helen demanded. The door to her private office had been duly slammed, in a manner consistent with the formal early moments of such conversations.

I smiled and took my seat in front of her massive mahogany desk. Helen, in accordance with the dictates of long-standing custom, did not take a seat but paced back and forth across the ample, well-carpeted corner office.

Something about this exchange was different from our past interviews, however. Helen was staring at me as though I had been imported from another dimension.

"What was I thinking about what, Helen?"

"About what?" she demanded, her voice rising a full octave. "About not returning my calls for two weeks! About ignoring my messages! About ignoring Donna's text messages! About leaving me to deal with half a dozen crises all on my own! About sabotaging the critical new Respect the Customer initiative, the initiative that is, as far as I can make out, the one and only thing that can save our operation right now! What the hell were you thinking about when you walked out on me at the very moment I needed you most? I tell you, Bruce, if you weren't my best friend, I'd fire you on the spot!"

The room was still for a moment as Helen waited for me to apologise, which is what I would certainly have done without the slightest hesitation two weeks earlier. I noticed a look of puzzled disorientation playing across Helen's face as it dawned on her that, for some inexplicable reason, I was not apologising. Then I saw her reposition her expression into the blank-stare, barely suppressed rage with which she met every perceived personal betrayal from an employee, ally, family member, or anyone else she deemed worthy of her own unique "good cop, bad cop in a single CEO" offensive. According to a script of long standing, I was now supposed to do something to keep her from getting worked up again, something that would bring back the Helen who asked me how my kids were doing, handed out big bonuses, and talked about where we were going to take the company together.

But I said nothing.

"Well?" she finally shouted, no longer able to contain herself. "Twenty-nine years I have been there for you! Twenty-nine years! And for what? So, I could watch you sailing off into the sunset while I was left down here on the ground to deal with the vultures circling around this company? Is that what our company means to you, Bruce?"

I took a deep breath.

XXIV:
R-E-S-P-E-C-T

"**H**ELEN," I SAID CALMLY, "I had a bit of a revelation while I was away."

A deafening silence, a silence of a completely unprecedented character, settled over the room. Helen stared at me as though I had been taken over by some alien intelligence—which, in a way, I had.

"You had what?"

"A revelation."

"What?"

"A revelation. About the respect initiative. Among other things. Would you like to hear it? It affects both of us, actually."

"Did you get hopped-up on some kind of medication in Hawaii that I need to know about?"

"No."

"Okay, Bruce, I give up. What's the freaking revelation?"

"It occurred to me that, around here, people ought to treat each other with respect. And I think that starts with the two of us. Could we agree on that as a standard for our own relationship first?"

She thought for a moment, sniffed, stared at me for a long moment, and then nodded warily, as if to see where this was all going.

"It's time for us to level with each other, Helen," I said. "We have a decision to make. I love you like a sister, but you need to know that I just plain can't do this anymore, not the way we've been doing it. If you don't accept some accountability for what's been happening around here, if you don't work with me to change the way we communicate with each other and with the rest of the company, if you and I can't find a way to change the rules by which we play...then I have to leave. It's as simple as that. I felt I owed it to you to tell you that in person, so that's what I'm doing. That's because, after all, I really do respect you, just like I am sure you can respect what I'm saying and why I'm saying it. I will stick around, but only if you let me make some changes here, changes that will affect our culture as an organisation."

Silence. Absolute, complete silence as Helen pondered the face of the man who was still (she realised) the very best, and perhaps only, true friend she had left in the building. Me.

Key cultural attributes must be consciously understood and agreed to by all they affect. They cannot be imposed from the outside of a relationship.

Finally, she said, "Listen, Bruce. If it's a choice between you leaving and you playing some new touchy-feely game about culture, fine, I'll play. We need you too much not to. You've got thirty days. Do what you want."

We had an agreement. That night, I sent out an e-mail to all our senior managers advising them to clear their schedules because we would be having an important meeting the following Monday. Helen would be in attendance.

XXV: IF

"So you're ready?" Sam Sherlock asked me over the phone. He was back in New York City, but he was keeping tabs on me and offering advice, as promised.

"As ready as I'll ever be, I imagine." I sighed into the hands-free mobile. I was driving to work, in the fast lane for some inexplicable reason, rushing to face a day that I had been trying to avoid thinking about all week.

"Don't forget to ask them for the numbers," Sam said. "And don't forget to pause for a nice long time after you say 'if.' Everything will work out just fine once you land the silence after that 'if' properly."

"I won't forget," I promised.

"Knock 'em dead," he advised. "And remember to take plenty of deep breaths."

"I will do my level best," I said.

XXVI:

U SUALLY, WHEN HELEN SHOWED UP for what she anticipated would be a difficult meeting with all our senior people, she started twisting an earring. It was a signal that she was in the mood to bite someone's head off, fire someone, or both. These highly visible encounters, well-known throughout the company, were Helen's favourite personal strategies for stress reduction. So it was with a familiar mix of tension, the barely suppressed desire to flee the premises, and a profound sense of career uncertainty that all the senior people in the organisation gathered in the main conference room. There they awaited their leader's next pronouncement, presumably about the much-ridiculed-in-private but much-praised-in-public, respect initiative.

Everyone was gathered around the same dreary conference table, the scene of so many humiliations and shouting matches in the past. Everyone was pretending to be unconcerned about whatever arbitrary career decapitation was about to be ordered. Everyone had the same implausible expression of mild amusement at the latest contrived small talk. Everyone was pretending not to watch the same massive door at the far end of the room, the point from which Helen customarily emerged, scowling, for these kinds of meetings. That huge, ornate, redwood-patterned door led directly to Helen's personal office. It was the cauldron from which countless molten temper tantrums had originated.

Presently Helen emerged from that door, eyes aflame, like the rock star she knew herself to be. She took her seat at the head of the conference room table, set down her cup of fresh-brewed Kopi Luwak coffee, cleared her throat (a well-established Pavlovian signal for "Be quiet now"), and began the meeting.

"I know we've been hitting some bumps in the road lately," she said. "So first and foremost, before we cover anything else, I just have to say that I need to be absolutely sure that everyone in this room is capable of maintaining focus, without getting distracted, so we can move on to the next phase of our growth. I am assuming that you can all handle that, and I am also assuming you are here at this company because this is where you want to be."

She stared pointedly at Dave Dude, who simply stared back with an ambiguous grin.

"If that's not the case," Helen intoned carefully and firmly, "then please feel free to talk to me personally after our session today."

A familiar cold silence gripped the room. Helen took another long, thoughtful sip of her coffee, then turned to me.

"Okay, Bruce, the floor is yours. Take it away." She then pulled out her phone and began to scan her latest emails.

XXVII:
BRUCE TAKES THE FLOOR

I BREATHED DEEPLY, STOOD UP, AND looked all around the conference room. A roomful of impossible-to-read faces stared back at me, each of them wondering, I supposed, what new, sadistic trick Helen had put me up to.

"I don't think I have to tell anyone in this room," I began, "that our company is facing some major challenges today. You have all been here long enough, and you have all invested enough of yourselves in this organisation, for me to be able to level with you. I've been looking over everything very carefully over the past few days, and I am here to tell you that we are going to get this ship righted, and we are going to get it righted quick. If we don't, there isn't going to be any ship for us to right."

Whether we realise it or not, culture is what drives everything else.

Everybody in the room, including Helen, looked as though I had just tried to spoon-feed them something off a hot stove.

"So believe me when I tell you that the reason I'm here with you today is that I truly believe that we can be a great company again if we make the right changes. I'm leading this meeting because Helen believes that too, and I know that she's eager for us to sort things out here and then move forward. I want to start out by saying how grateful I am to Helen for agreeing to let me guide us through a process that will be difficult at times. But even though it won't be easy, it will definitely help us to deliberately improve our bottom line by changing our working culture for the better. Now, maybe you're wondering: Why are we doing this? Why even bother looking at the culture? Shouldn't we be looking at more pressing matters? No. Because, whether we realise it or not, culture is what drives everything else."

With that, I pulled out a deck of blank index cards, pulled off the plastic, and passed out a card to each person in the room, starting with Helen.

"So let me ask each of you a question," I said. "If the culture in this workplace were to be improved to be as good as it realistically could be, how much of an impact do you think that would have on people's performance and productivity? Zero percent? One percent? Fifty percent? Take an educated guess, and write the number down on the card I just gave you. You don't have to put your name on it. I'll be collecting the cards in just a moment."

People pulled out pens and pencils obediently. Some gazed philosophically at the cards for a while. For the longest time, nothing happened. Some of those in attendance stared noncommittally at the ceiling, while others looked for the right answer on the backs of their hands.

> Ask yourself (and all the senior members of your team): If the culture in your organisation were to be improved so that it was as good as it realistically could be, how much of an impact do you think that would have on everyone's performance and productivity? Assign a realistic percentage for the increase.

"There is no way to get a wrong answer on this," I assured the group. "Just jot down the first number that comes to mind and then turn the card over, facedown."

More silence. I found myself wishing that Sam Sherlock were doing this.

> Nine out of ten senior managers believe that a realistic improvement in their own workplace culture would result in productivity improvements of at least 20 percent.

Finally, Helen picked up the card, jotted down a number, and put the card face down in front of her. Everyone else followed suit. As soon as they were done, I collected all the cards and shuffled them, making sure people saw me to ensure anonymity.

"There's been some interesting research done on this. The researchers asked over five hundred people, in all kinds of different industries and across continents, that same question I just asked you. And you know what they found out? When you asked senior managers that question, nine out of ten of them said that improving the culture would lead to improvements in productivity of at least twenty percent.

"Now let's look at your responses."

XXVIII:

BY THE NUMBERS

I PUT THE NUMBERS FROM THE cards on the whiteboard.

"Well, we can see from what I've written here that our numbers are pretty much in line with that research. Here we all are, managers and executives, and here are our numbers ranging from a low of fifteen percent to a high of one hundred percent. The average from the people in this room would look to be north of thirty percent."

The team nodded in agreement—all except Helen, who had gone back to staring at her text messages.

"What's really interesting," I said, "is the research also acquired responses from nonmanagers. They found that almost seventy percent of employees without managerial responsibility felt that realistically improving company culture would bump productivity up by at least fifty percent."

A hush fell over the room.

"So there is a potential breakthrough in productivity here, sitting right under our noses. There is significant unrealised capacity waiting for us. And it seems to me, given the research, that our own employees would probably see the potential for even larger increases in productivity than the numbers that we just wrote down. *If...*"

I played out the silence for as long as I could, just as Sam had suggested that I do at this point in the discussion.

To gain maximum value from UGRs, your organisation must proceed through a five-step process:

Envision: Clarify the key cultural attributes (KCAs) necessary for the organisation's future success.

Assess: Evaluate the current culture in terms of the KCAs and implement improvements based on that evaluation.

Teach: Familiarise as many people as possible, and especially leaders, with the UGRs concept.

"*If* we do what other great companies in other industries who faced big trouble and turned themselves around have done.

"*If* we do what Apple and Zappos and Disney have done, and continually redo, year after year.

"*If* we find our way through to the only credible way I know of to do more with less in one hell of a hurry, which is to make sure people care more about what they're doing.

"*If* we choose to take conscious control of our own culture and design it and implement it in a way that supports us and supports our goals.

"Because if you ask me, my friends, this is our last chance. How else can we realistically expect to pull ourselves out of the hole we're in if we don't improve our productivity by between twenty and fifty percent? And sooner rather than later. If anyone has a better plan, I am all ears. But I honestly believe this is our best, and perhaps our only, option to pull this company out of its nose dive."

No answer came back—which is what Sam told me to expect.

"All right then. So let's begin, right here and right now. There are five steps for us to work through over the next few weeks, all based on a concept I'll be sharing with you soon called UGRs—or 'Unwritten Ground Rules.' The first of those steps is for us to *Envision* the kind of culture we really need to be truly successful."

Involve: Involve people in creating and prioritising aspirational, positive UGRs—linked to the KCAs or value statements—by which they would like to char acterise the organisation into the future.

Embed: Identify and implement strategies to embed the aspirational, positive UGRs.

XXIX

I SAW A COUPLE OF SENIOR people glancing over to Helen to see whether she would stop me, contradict me, or arch her eyebrows in disgust (a favourite "silent veto" tactic of hers). But she was still engrossed in her iPhone, a signal that everyone in the room knew from long experience should be translated as "I am far too important for this discussion. Proceed without me, and I will object if I hear a problem."

"What 'Envision' really means," I continued, "is that we are all going to have to understand the specific cultural attributes that we are going to need here, not just to overcome our present challenges but to compete and thrive in the long term while also making this a great place to work.

> People will only support that which they help to create.

"We have got to decide for ourselves whether we are now operating under the right ground rules for our organisation, and, if not, what those ground rules ought to be.

"For that, I will need the help of each and every person in this room. I want you to help make sure that we get this right. We cannot do this without you. And we cannot do this without you taking your people through this as well."

I stopped for a moment to let that much sink in, then proceeded.

"Our job is a big one. We are here to deliberately create and follow a new and more productive working culture, a culture that is consciously designed to get us where we need to go. Every truly successful organisation has carefully chosen specific cultural attributes that it not only expects its people to play by, but also talks about regularly and reinforces. This kind of cultural change is more than a new way to talk and a new set of posters for us to put up. It is either going to be the key to our success or the reason this company disintegrates. And I, for one, am not willing to watch it disintegrate."

> The goal of this process is to deliberately create and follow a new and more productive working culture, a culture that is consciously designed to get the organisation to where it needs to go, while also making it a great place to work. .

Helen looked up for a moment from her iPhone, then nodded and went back to writing an e-mail.

"There should be a clear map," I went on, "a map that tells everyone on the team exactly where north is on our compass. For about five years now, we've been telling you that north sounded like this: communication, respect, integrity, and excellence. Those value statements, although they were well intentioned, didn't really gain traction. On a practical, organisational level, those four words, on their own, just were not doing a good-enough job of creating or supporting the culture that this organisation needs to succeed.

"For one thing, we didn't attach any benchmarks that would allow us all to agree on whether we were getting closer to, or farther away from, the goal of living these values on a day-to-day basis. What's more, we didn't have any meaningful discussions about what they actually meant. As a result, we have not managed to align these values with our day-to-day interactions, and we haven't been doing a very good job of living up to them. That's the reality, whether or not we choose to say as much out loud. That's why communication, respect, integrity, and excellence haven't gotten the job done for us. Put simply, the values haven't become our behaviours."

Helen stared at me like a wounded boar pondering an angle of attack but held her peace. The rest of the gathering held its collective breath.

"It gets worse. We've repeated those four words for so long, and in so many different settings, with so many different purposes, that they have not only stopped being effective tools for us but have become obstacles to creating the culture we need if we want to succeed in the marketplace. We sometimes even acted like we never cared what those words meant to our employees. They are now nothing more than shorthand for a dysfunctional set of behaviours. It's not the values per se that have been the problem, but the fact that they haven't been lived. And this has created negativity and cynicism. We don't necessarily have to abandon those words publicly, but as managers, we do need to stop acting as though repeating them earnestly is the solution to the problems we face here.

> It is just as important to establish and manage cultural rules as it is to manage rules for things like finance, safety, and legal liability. We often fail to manage culture because we fall into the trap of managing the things that are easiest to manage and monitor.

"We need to face facts. What we are doing now to manage our culture is not working. And we really do need to change the culture if we plan on surviving."

I noticed everyone glancing surreptitiously at Helen, whose expression remained impossible to read and whose focus on her text messages was once again complete and unyielding.

"So," I continued, "what we are going to ask you to do today is to help us begin the job of digging a little deeper. We are going to ask you to help us all get greater clarity on exactly what kind of culture we all need to be able to work in, day in and day out, to achieve success.

The first step in the process is to pose the question "What are the key cultural attributes we need in place for us to be truly successful?"—and then discuss that question in depth.

"Now, the whole reason I am here talking to you this morning is that I believe we all need to do a better job of managing the culture of this organisation. Let me tell you briefly why I feel that way.

"If someone in our organisation does something wrong when it comes to financial protocols, actions swiftly kick in. An investigation takes place, and, if the breaches are serious enough, the guilty party is reprimanded or fired.

"If someone at our company behaves in a way that puts his or her own or others' safety and well-being at risk, or exposes our company to unacceptable levels of legal liability, there again, actions kick in. The responsible people in our organisation will review what's happened, and again, the guilty party will be reprimanded, retrained, or fired.

Developing a list of key cultural attributes should involve the senior leadership team but can include all employees.

"But what if someone acts in a way that is not consistent with the kind of culture we need to be successful? What if someone begins behaving in ways that are just not consistent with our desired culture?

"Our actions need to kick in there too, because not managing the culture is at least as big a threat to the company as not managing financial protocols, at least as big a threat as not managing legal liability. If this is to work, even we at the top have to buy into this and implement it.

"Maybe you're wondering: How did we get here? Well, many leaders, including me, including Helen, can fall into the trap of managing the things that are easier to manage and monitor. Someone acting outside the financial rules is relatively easy to track—although we recognise there are complexities in many contexts! - and therefore relatively easy to manage. And while getting people to adhere consistently to legal liability standards may be difficult, the breaches are relatively easy to spot, and follow-up procedures are relatively easy to construct.

> Don't discount yourself from this process if you've focused seriously and strongly on a clearly defined and agreed upon set of values, as these can be used in place of KCAs.

"But managing culture is much more difficult. That's why we need your help today. To get started, I want you to choose a partner and work together to answer the sentence I'm going to write on the whiteboard right now."

I uncapped a whiteboard marker and wrote the following words on the board:

What are the KEY CULTURAL ATTRIBUTES we need in place for us to be truly successful?

FILLING IN THE BLANKS:

THEY STARED AT THE WHITEBOARD as though I had written my message in a foreign language—which I suppose I had. The very first time Sam Sherlock shared these same concepts with me, on our long plane trip to Hawaii, his ideas had seemed like incomprehensible, touchy-feely mush—which was undoubtedly how they seemed to our senior executives now. I knew it would take lots of engagement, discussion, and reinforcement for these concepts to take root.

"Okay, guys," I asked, "can anyone give me an example of a cultural attribute?"

There was a brief, uneasy pause, followed by the familiar sight of Dave Dude's hand shooting up in the air. He was always the first to speak in a meeting or training session. In fact, he was a lot like the fourth grader I had been, the kind who had decided, correctly, that they were more likely to get a good grade in class by being the first to suggest a possible answer than by waiting until they understood what the hell the teacher was talking about.

"Dave?" I said.

"Profit," said Dave Dude, the hotshot consultant. "Profit is the most important cultural attribute, or at least it needs to be. If a company doesn't take care of the bottom line, it is doomed."

"Actually, that's not really the answer I was looking for, Dave," I said as politely as I could. "Profit is not a cultural attribute. Profit is an outcome. A cultural attribute describes something we do within our culture. Anyone else?"

> Profit is not a cultural attribute. Profit is an outcome.

There was another long pause. Donna Messwidme, Helen's personal assistant, raised her hand from the very back of the room.

"Yes, Donna?"

"How about communication?"

"It's a good beginning," I said, "but communication is what we call a 'suitcase word.'"

"What does that mean?" Donna asked.

"It means we need to unpack it a little bit before we can understand what it is about communication that we value as being important around here," I said.

Donna thought for a moment, then said, "I guess we all need to do a better job of communicating openly and honestly. And we shouldn't ever be penalised for trying to do that."

"Excellent start. Now we're getting somewhere!" I said.

Out of the corner of my eye, I saw that Helen was staring philosophically at her coffee cup, her face an unreadable mask. Perhaps she had realised that what Donna had had the courage to say out loud was not only true but was also one of our biggest problems as an organisation. Yet she said nothing, and, once she had taken a sip, she stayed focused like a laser beam on her iPhone.

"So: *Why* is open and honest communication going to be so important to the success of our organisation?" I asked.

"Open communication at all times is going to be absolutely critical for us if we are going to fix what's broken here and move forward," said Burt Blunt, the VP of accounting. "We have a lot of different little silos doing a lot of different things, and there are not clear lines of communication for handling issues and solving problems that affect more than one of those little fiefdoms. We have to start speaking and using the same language."

A few more people spoke up over the next few minutes; each agreed with what Donna or Burt had had to say. Helen maintained her stony silence.

"Good job, everyone," I said. "Let's agree that this is the first of the key cultural attributes necessary for our future success. You've gotten a sense of how this works. Now it's time for us to break into smaller teams so we can find out what other KCAs we should be looking at."

XXXI: SURVIVE AND THRIVE

I T TOOK A WHILE FOR each of the teams to come up with its "long list" of cultural attributes and even more time for the group as a whole to reach consensus on what the right "short list" of KCAs were. All sin all, there was about two hours of healthy, vigorous debate. Helen did not participate in that debate.

A general agreement emerged. I noticed with some relief that, although I had done little to shape the content of the discussions that followed our initial meeting, the list of cultural attributes our senior managers had identified dealt with the same big issues that had been troubling me since the day I left for Honolulu—and, truth be told, for years before that.

We had already agreed that "open communication at all times" was our first item.

"'Genuine commitment to customer service' has to matter to us more than it does right now," Valerie Brightly from marketing said on behalf of her team. "It's too easy right now for people to make excuses for not delivering what they need to deliver to customers, when they need to deliver it. We don't yet have a culture that celebrates customer service and rewards it, and we are going to have to change that if we want to survive and compete in the current environment."

"'Respect for people across all boundaries' is absolutely essential," Martha Mothering from human resources suggested. "We talk about it a lot, but we haven't yet figured out a way to live it as a daily reality."

"'Displaying initiative and innovation at all times' is something we must improve constantly in an ever-more-competitive marketplace," Paul Prototype from R&D insisted. "People need to take ownership of problems and issues and then feel authorised and empowered to take the steps necessary to solve those problems. They should get praise and be rewarded when they do that, even if they make a mistake or two along the way."

"'Accountability for fulfilling commitments made' is another big issue," Frank Flowchart from operations maintained. "If we aren't willing to stand up and accept responsibility in our relationships with each other, there's no way on earth we are going to be able to give our customers the level of accountability they expect."

"'Quality interdepartmental relationships' have to bring everything together for us," Jack Oldschool, a veteran sales manager, advised. "We need a sense of everybody being on the same team, of people working for the common good. We used to have that value as a major asset back in the days when we were getting this company off the ground. I'm not so sure we have it as strongly right now. There's a sense of everyone looking out for his or her own interests first. We need to regroup around the idea of identifying and acting on the interests of the team."

> Identify an initial list of between four and eight KCAs that your organisation needs to have in order to survive and thrive in its current and future environment.

XXXII:

DISCUSSING THAT WHICH IS UNDISCUSSED

"**T**HAT'S AWESOME WORK, GUYS—AND I couldn't agree more with what you've come up with," I said. "Now let's quantify this a little.

"Just a little while back, we all agreed that there is more than thirty percent in unrealised potential performance gains just waiting to be captured—and maybe even greater gains—*if* we get our culture to the point where it supports us and is productive. So, my question for you now is: How much of that thirty percent would we be able to see and experience for ourselves, *if,* we actually lived by all six of these key cultural attributes?"

They thought about that for a moment, and then Burt Blunt said, "Maybe all thirty. Maybe more."

"I agree," I said. "I think we now have at least six key cultural attributes that have the potential to make it possible for us to become the kind of company we need to be—and create. Let me suggest right now that the only way we can begin the process of living by these cultural attributes, which we all seem to agree are important to use, is for us to take a closer look at the culture we're living by right now. And to do that, we are going to need to look at the concept of Unwritten Ground Rules."

I pulled out my marker and wrote on the whiteboard:

Unwritten Ground Rules, or UGRs, are the undiscussed rules that drive behaviour in organisations—including ours. They are people's perceptions of "the way we do things around here."

"The key word there is 'undiscussed,'" I said. "UGRs are seldom talked about openly. Yet they regulate just about all our interactions in the workplace. In fact, it's the UGRs in any company that constitute its true culture. Examples of UGRs in companies include:

- At our meetings, it isn't worth complaining because nothing will get done.
- The only time anyone gets spoken to by the boss is when something is wrong.
- The company talks about good customer service, but we know they don't really mean it, so we don't really have to worry about it.

"So if we want to understand what is actually happening with our culture, we've got to do some exploring. We've got to identify the UGRs that we're playing by right now. Because they're not supporting us."

Dave Dude nodded solemnly.

"Realistically, you can't expect to implement key cultural attributes without doing some work up front," I said. "You can't expect to make positive cultural changes without identifying the culture that's already in place. Specifically, we need to figure out what our prevailing UGRs are in each of the six KCAs you have worked so hard to come up with today. If you think about it, you'll realise that we can't possibly succeed in incorporating these KCAs, or changing our outcomes, or improving our productivity, if we don't know what the culture looks like right now across these six dimensions. And that means getting the entire company to look closely at the Unwritten Ground Rules we are all playing by—right here, right now. This leads us to the second step: Assess."

At this point, Helen looked up from her iPhone and said she needed ten minutes for a break.

It seemed to me we were on the verge of either a breakthrough or a breakdown. I chose to assume it was the former and found a corner of the room where I could work uninterrupted for a few precious moments. I knew that I had a very narrow window in which to work.

XXXIII: GETTING YOUR ASSESS IN GEAR

FOR STEP TWO OF THE process—the "Assess" phase—I had to craft six special sentences called lead-in sentences, each of which had to connect to one of the six KCAs we had just identified. These sentences would be the subject of our next discussion—and, eventually, we would ask the entire company to complete the sentences online.

After some intense wordsmithing and a brief call to Sam Sherlock to review my lead-in sentences, here's what I came up with:

> For *open communication*: Around here, when you need information to solve a problem...

> For *genuine commitment to customer service*: Around here, customers are...

Creating the lead-in sentences that will mark the beginning of the assess step is both an art and a science. It requires time, patience, and a good deal of practice. These incomplete sentences must match up with the KCAs identified as necessary for the organisation's future success and must be completed by all stakeholders for later analysis. The lead-in sentences are among the most important tools in managing your organisation's culture. For help crafting the right lead-in sentences, contact us at www.ugrs.net.

For *respect for people across all boundaries*: Around here, people are treated...

In crafting lead-in sentences for the Assess phase, be sure to avoid sentences like "Around here, quality is..." because this kind of lead-in sentence invites a definition. It gives people an excuse to go off on their own little tangent, and maybe even deliver a lecture on a favourite subject, rather than inspire a productive conversation about "the way we currently do things around here."

For *displaying initiative and innovation at all times*: Around here, when you come up with a new idea...

For *accountability for fulfilling commitments made*: Around here, when someone says he or she will do something...

For *quality interdepartmental relationships*: Around here, when it comes to dealing with other departments...

I saved my file of completed lead-in sentences. Then I quickly populated the draft forms that I'd set up earlier that morning and printed up one copy per person before going into the hallway to get a drink of water from the cooler. There, I saw Helen.

XXXIV:

"OKAY, I GOT YOUR LITTLE hint about communication," she said in a hoarse whisper. "Let's say, for the sake of argument, that you're right. Let's say I've neglected the communication piece. Let's say I do need to mind my p's and q's and listen once in a while if I want to settle the inmates down and keep them from taking over the asylum. Can we be finished now?"

"Not by a long shot," I said. "We're just getting started. And by the way, it's not a little hint. And it's not just for you. It's for all of us. It's for our survival."

"You've got a nerve, Bruce," she said, her jaw set.

"I'm taking responsibility for the things I've helped to screw up, Helen," I whispered. "I'm doing what I think is right, but I can't do it if you spend the whole session staring at your iPhone. If you don't want me working to save what we've built together, let me know, because believe me, if I'm doing this all on my own, I'm ready to hit the road."

"All right, all right, calm down," she said, a little more loudly than absolutely necessary, and gestured that I should follow her. Apparently, we were headed toward her office for a private strategy session, even though our break had already stretched to ten full minutes. "You know what would make me feel a little better about this company's survival?"

"What's that, Helen?"

She had opened the door to her office and was gesturing for me to enter. "If we could get the backstabbers and traitors taken care of by legal," she said, "and I want them working on it now, starting Monday morning at eight a.m. sharp. So we don't have to worry about losing any more clients. And I think you know who I'm talking about."

Before we could close the door, we heard a familiar voice from the hall: "Backstabber? Traitor? Is that what I am?"

It was Dave Dude, who emerged from around the corner unexpectedly, probably looking for me. Five seconds later and her door would have been closed, the remark unheard, the scene unplayed. As it was, time had frozen, and Dave Dude was staring a hole in the raw air.

"Let me tell you something, Helen," Dave said slowly and carefully. "I joined this company with good intentions. I wanted to help you begin a new chapter in this little book you're writing. But I made a mistake, a big one. I listened to you when you were saying whatever had to be said to get me to sign on the bottom line. I listened to you when you said you wanted to hear about new ideas. I believed you. Now, I don't know exactly why, but for some reason, I was back on board with this sorry operation after that little session we just had in there. Maybe it seemed to me like someone was finally going to walk his talk. But when you talk behind my back, it reminds me why I soured on this place. I have already spoken to my attorney about that non-compete clause you and I negotiated when you were hustling me like I was the next big thing, trying to get me to put my name on your company, and he has assured me that I am good to go. As in take my clients and leave. I am just one decision away from doing what I've been thinking about for some time—which is take my clients, start my own company, and run for the horizon—then you won't have to worry about this little backstabber, this little traitor, anymore. But you will have to worry about whether I beat this exhausted company of yours into the ground. Because I will. So be careful, be very careful, Helen. I'll see you back in the conference room. Should be an interesting session."

And with that, he turned on his heel and walked away.

XXXV: AN ALLIANCE

HELEN WAS UNFAZED, AS USUAL, and had more ideas to bounce off me and more initiatives to discuss. Our ten-minute break had, by now, stretched to half an hour. I called Donna and asked her to make our long absence sound like a brainstorming session. She tried. Back in the conference room, though, after Helen told me to go on in and start without her, I found that everyone was still milling around, pretending not to look for Helen.

I sat down with Dave Dude.

"Dave," I said in a low voice, "I need for you to know something, and I need to make sure you hear it from me. But it's confidential, so we need to find a quiet place to talk. Have you got a moment for me?"

"Sure," Dave whispered, nodding. "We seem to be on an extended pause. Let's go in my office. It's quieter there."

Once we arrived, he offered me a coffee, but I declined politely. "I'm trying to cut down on my caffeine intake, plus we need to get back and get the session rolling" I said.

"What's on your mind, Bruce?"

"Look," I said. "I know you are on the brink of quitting this place so you can open up your own operation, and just between you and me, I don't blame you one bit for wanting to do that. In fact, if I can get your agreement to keep this next part confidential, I have something that I'd like you to know about the timing here."

"I'm all ears," said Dave, nodding. "And yes, whatever you say stays between you and me."

"Thank you. You've had as much as you can take from Helen," I said. "I know that. What you need to know is that I have too. If I can't get Helen's attention on this cultural change, if I can't get her to buy into what we've started here with everything she's got, then I am out of here too. Because, Dave, I have concluded that if we do tomorrow what we did yesterday, then our future is history.

"Now the thing is, Dave," I continued, "I've put in too much blood, toil, tears, and sweat to just walk away from this company. I know Helen and I think it's possible that she can change, once she realises what the stakes are."

> Build strategic alliances in support of the UGR process.

"If you say so," he said.

"And finally," I went on, "I need to ask you a favour. I need two weeks before you make the next move. Fourteen calendar days, starting tomorrow morning. During this time, I also need your full support in making this work. I need you to throw your weight in behind me so that we can lead this change together. Then, if you still think the working environment is not moving in the right direction at that point, after I've given this initiative everything I've got, then go ahead and leave. But I need two weeks from you to try to put all the puzzle pieces together. And if, after that, you're looking for someone to help in getting this new company started, I'll be happy to be that person. Because I'll be looking for a job too. Can you make sure to keep that message in mind, as well?"

"Okay. You can count on that," he said.

"Until we get this all straightened out," I said, "I think it's best if you and I proceed discreetly, on the assumption that this conversation never happened."

"What conversation?" Dave asked.

XXXVI:

HELEN AT THE BRINK

HELEN WAS STILL BACK IN her inner sanctum, behind the big mahogany desk, staring at her hands. Donna, her trusted assistant of nineteen long years, walked in searchingly, then stopped abruptly when she saw her boss in this unprecedented position.

"Everyone's looking for you, Helen," she said quietly, after giving her a moment. "They're ready to start when you are. It's time."

Those two words from Donna always meant reality was waiting. Helen nodded, got up, and headed for the conference room, and Donna followed with the studied obedience of one accustomed, from long service, to the art of leading by following.

XXXVII:
THE WILSON FACTOR

ONCE HELEN OPENED THE BIG door that all eyes were pretending not to watch, once she made her customary long strides to the big chair at the head of the conference table, she saw these words written on the whiteboard:

> *He who rejects change is the architect of decay. The only human institution which rejects progress is the cemetery.*
> *—Harold Wilson*

"We are here to talk about change," I said to the assembled group, all of whom had stopped their bustling and chatting now that Helen was in the room. "And as I said before the break, the next step in our change is called *Assess*. That's exactly what we are going to do. Assess the UGRs we are currently playing by, even if we have never said those rules out loud before."

I then passed out copies of the printed sheets I'd picked up on my way back to the room. Each sheet read:

A CULTURE TURNED

1. Around here, when you need information to solve a problem...

_____

_____

_____

➡️ | **Impact of this:**
Positive ❑
Neutral ❑
Negative ❑

2. Around here, customers are...

_____

_____

_____

➡️ | **Impact of this:**
Positive ❑
Neutral ❑
Negative ❑

3. Around here, people are treated...

_____

_____

_____

➡️ | **Impact of this:**
Positive ❑
Neutral ❑
Negative ❑

4. Around here, when you come up with a new idea...

_____

_____

_____

➡️ | **Impact of this:**
Positive ❑
Neutral ❑
Negative ❑

5. Around here, when someone says he or she will do something...

_____

_____

_____

➡️ | **Impact of this:**
Positive ❑
Neutral ❑
Negative ❑

6. Around here, when it comes to dealing with other departments...

_____

_____

_____

➡️ | **Impact of this:**
Positive ❑
Neutral ❑
Negative ❑

"I don't want these sheets back from you. They're just meant to give you a preview of the exercise that you—and everyone else in the company—will be completing online over the next few days. You may have noticed that each of the sentences on this sheet connects to one of the key cultural attributes we have identified today. You will also notice that none of the sentences is complete. They're what are known as *lead-in sentences*. They're an extremely important tool that will allow us to complete a process called a UGRs Stock Take, or inventory. After you complete each sentence, you should self-categorise the response you've just given as positive, neutral, or negative in terms of its overall impact on the company.

> Once you have identified the right key cultural attributes (KCAs) for organisational success, the next logical question is: How close are we right now to living and working according to those KCAs? This is what you learn during the second phase, *Assess.*

"What I want you all to do tonight, in the privacy of your own home, is log on, fill in the blanks, and pull no punches. I want you to complete these sentences anonymously based on where we are, right now, today.

> All the lead-in sentences must be completed and submitted anonymously.

"I am not inviting you to be negative here. I am inviting you to be honest. If your response happens to be negative, that's fine; write it that way. But equally, if your response happens to be positive, use that as well.

"Now it's possible that as you consider each lead-in sentence, you will think to yourself, 'It depends.' If that happens, then that's what you write—making sure you explain what you mean.

"We will meet again here Friday at nine a.m. to review the results. Please, if you remember nothing else about how to fill out this online form, remember this: do not write what you think Helen or I want to hear, because if you do that, none of us will be able to get a clear sense of where you think we are right now in terms of the extent to which we are living the cultural attributes you have helped us to identify today. Of course, Helen and I will be completing this as well, just as you're doing.

It is common to do the Stock Take via e-mail or online, but it can also be done manually, with paper and pen (while maintaining anonymity, of course).

"A final reminder: each person completing this online assessment must do so entirely on his or her own. Thank you for all your help today! We'll see you when we reconvene."

XXXVIII:

MONDAY AHEAD

EARLY FRIDAY MORNING, HELEN RAN her weary-looking eyes over the columns of text, sighed with every page she turned, and muttered incomprehensibly to herself every once in a while. I sat in the seat across from her long mahogany desk, watching her patiently. I noticed that she seemed to wince slightly as she made her way from the end of one carefully framed paragraph to the beginning of the next.

Finally, she reached the end of the lengthy printout that I had prepared for her.

"This is a disaster," she said, tossing the sheaf to her desktop. "There's no possible way for us to fix this in time."

"I disagree," I said, summoning an infusion of confidence that was on loan from Sam Sherlock, which I hoped, with every fibre of my being, was justified.

The printout Helen had been wrestling with was the complete UGRs Stock Take, incorporating all the completed lead-in sentences of all the employees of the Very Important Corporation. Truth be told, I had very little reason to challenge Helen's initial assessment of the completed sentences as "disastrous." They certainly were a disaster if we made no attempt to learn from them.

"My day was lousy enough already. Why the hell did you show me this?" Helen demanded.

"Because, Helen," I said calmly, "I felt you had a right to see it before we start the analysis of the Stock Take with the entire management team. I showed it to you because, if you plan on leading an effective turnaround here, you should know what kinds of things people really say around the water cooler, what kinds of things they say when they get home, what kinds of things they think about all day long. What you just read on those sheets are the real rules our organisation is playing by, whether we like it or not. In fact, right now, these

> Even if you're asked to do so, don't reveal your own answers to the Stock Take.

are the only rules that actually matter until we start learning about them and changing them. I showed them to you because I believe these UGRs can be changed if we look closely at the reality of what it's like to work here."

Helen stared at me, waiting for me to blink. It was a decades-old trick that had often worked on me, but I saw it coming this time, thankfully, and held her gaze until she looked away.

"Let me ask you one question," she said at last.

"Yes?"

"Did you complete the Stock Take?"

"I did."

"And which of these sentences were yours?" she asked.

"I'm not telling," I said, smiling.

XXXIX:
HELEN STEPS UP

MONDAY MORNING, THE ENTIRE GROUP assembled in the conference room once again, a sense of excitement and anticipation hanging in the air. I was surprised to notice Dave Dude sitting directly across from me and glancing at me, for the tiniest moment, with something that looked similar to hope. If it was hope for the resurrection of this company, then it was a hope held, like mine, against all better judgement. Up to this point, all I could tell for sure that I had accomplished was getting Helen's attention about something that I thought was important. Yet that was a start. And wasn't Dave's glance at me across the table a start too, an indication of something positive?

"Welcome back," I said. "You guys did exactly as I asked, and I really want to thank everyone for that. I can't promise that what follows will be easy to listen to, easy to read, or easy to fix. What I can promise, though, is that it will be real. And real is what we need right now. It's time to hear how people finished our lead-in sentences. The first of those sentences, as I am sure most of you remember, is..."

I counted the length of the pause in seconds. Ten. Eleven. Twelve.

The silence hung there for an achingly long moment; I waited to see who would fill it in. It was an old trick of Sam's that he had e-mailed me that morning. The person who spoke up first, Sam advised, was likely to be someone willing to take a stand, someone who would take the lead and be publicly accountable for making positive change happen within the organisation.

"Around here, when you need information to solve a problem..." Helen volunteered, finally.

How about that, I thought. *She steps up at last.*

I flicked on the projector I had linked to my laptop. The screen leapt to life.

"Now, since we last met, I've analysed the way everyone in the company completed that sentence. Some of the responses to the lead-ins were negative in nature – meaning that the given UGRs have a negative impact on our performance. Other responses were rated as positive - meaning that the given UGRs have a positive impact on performance. Yet others were neutral. Everyone categorised each of their responses as having a positive, negative or neutral impact as they filled out the online questionnaire. So let me ask you to make a prediction: How do you think the answers broke down?"

Without waiting for an answer, I continued. "I want you to give me three numbers. What percentage of the responses will be positive? What percentage will be neutral? And what percentage will be negative? I'm afraid Helen doesn't get to guess, since I've already shown her the pie charts."

The group laughed nervously.

"I can give you guys a big, fat hint, though," Helen said conspiratorially. "It isn't pretty."

This produced a bigger and (it seemed to me) healthier laugh.

I brought up a PowerPoint page that held a single empty pie chart. The eyes of everyone in the group shifted instantly to the screen.

"In a moment," I said, "I'll be showing you the overall results, including the comments made by the rest of our people. Ready? Okay, guys what will the numbers show? Anyone brave enough to take a guess? Give me your predictions for the percentage of positive, neutral, and negative responses, in that order."

Donna Messwidme said, "I'll give it a go."

"Donna—what's your prediction?"

"Thirty percent positive, twenty percent neutral, and fifty percent negative," she said boldly.

"Thirty, twenty, fifty," I said, trying to mirror her optimism. "Let's see how that matches up with what we actually did."

I hit the clicker, and the pie chart suddenly filled the screen with colour. A little gasp worked its way through the room.

"Here's what we actually heard from everybody," I said soberly. "Fourteen percent positive, nine percent neutral, and seventy-seven percent negative."

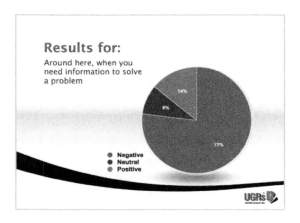

"Now, what I want you to notice is that, in our case, negative and neutral add up to eighty-six percent for this lead-in sentence, which we might refer to as 'non-positive.' And I really think it does make sense for us to look at it that way. After all, if any of our UGRs are not clearly positive, then it's obviously not moving us in the direction we want to go. If it's not positive, it's not the way we want it to be.

"Is anyone curious to see what the numbers look like when you break down all six of the lead-in sentences?"

"Why the hell not," said Dave Dude. "We're gluttons for punishment." This brought another laugh from the group.

I worked my way through the (equally daunting) results of the remaining lead-in sentences, discussing each. This took about ten minutes and yielded the complete six–pie chart slide that Sam called the "dashboard." Here's what it looked like:

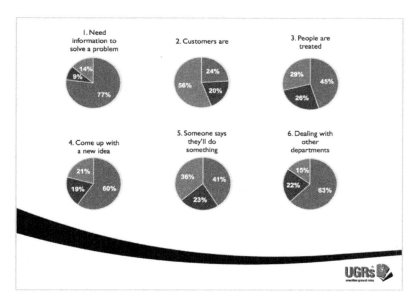

"Our job," I said, "is pretty straightforward. We want to get all six of the pie charts on this chart to show improved positive numbers every single quarter, and then keep them trending in a positive direction. And we need your help to do it."

I removed a large manila envelope from my briefcase and held it up for all to see. "Now, in this envelope, I have a printout of some of the responses that we received to each of the lead-in sentences. I'm going to be breaking our group into six subgroups now, and then each of the subgroups will receive an envelope with the responses for a particular lead-in. What I want you to do is take just a few minutes to read the completed sentences. That will not only give you a sense of our current UGRs, it will also tell you how close or how far away we are from actually living the KCA that the lead-in sentence connects to. Read all the responses carefully, and then take a few minutes to get ready to deliver a report back to the group as a whole. In that report, I want you to do two things.

"First, I want you to give us a rundown on the general themes and messages you saw in the completed lead-in sentences you read. So, what are the positive UGRs saying? What are the neutral UGRs saying? What are the negative UGRs saying? Get a very clear sense of what all those trends are, and be ready to discuss them, because your subgroup is the only one that's going to read those particular lead-in sentences and see how they were completed.

"And second, I want you to think about the way our people as a whole are responding to the exercise, and then give our company a number between minus ten and plus ten that we'll call the 'performance impact score' based on the responses you just read. In other words, assume that all the completed lead-in sentences are an accurate reflection of our current culture in this particular area. Let's say you're looking at the first sentence—then what is the impact on performance across *all* the responses you read about communication on our bottom line? So if you think there's no impact, you would give

> The performance impact score is the answer to the question "If that is what the culture is really like here, with its mixture of positives and neutrals and negatives, what is the impact on the bottom line, on a scale of minus ten to ten?"

those responses a collective zero. On the other hand, if you think the responses have got a slightly positive impact on our bottom line, you might give them a plus two or a plus three. And if you think that, collectively, it's got a huge negative impact on our bottom line, you might give them a minus seven. This number is called the performance impact score, so it's not about one person just completing one sentence. It's about the impact that the UGRs that you see evidence of from this Stock Take are currently having on our organisation's performance.

"As I've said, each small group will have the responsibility of analysing the collection of responses to just *one* lead-in sentence. When that is done, we'll meet back here to give one another feedback so that it will then be as though everyone has read all the responses for each lead-in sentence. We'll reconvene here after lunch. On your mark, get set, go!"

Remember, giving a "zero" performance impact score is a totally legitimate option. Even if a response sounds negative, you might conclude that it won't actually have any impact on your organisation's performance.

XI

XL:

MUCH TO HIS SURPRISE, DAVE found himself chosen to work (with Donna Messwidme and me) in Helen's group. Helen had been designated the leader of the group. I had made a promise to myself to say as little as possible.

"I guess I'm supposed to read this instruction sheet to you guys before we begin," Helen said, "so here goes."

Thank you so much for taking part in the vital work we are doing this morning. It is extremely important for us to be willing to identify what the current UGRs really are. You have shown no small amount of courage and commitment by showing up here today. Here are a few procedural points you and the team should keep in mind before getting started.

1. First and foremost, please be sure to read all the responses to the lead-in sentences you have been given. As you will see, they are bunched into the categories "positive," "neutral," and "negative," as indicated by the person who completed each sentence – based on the impact that that UGR is having on our performance right now. Of

course, it's tempting to skip over the positives and neutrals in order to get to the negatives, which often carry strong emotion for both the writer and the reader. Please don't do that. You need to listen carefully to all three. If you read each response before discussing any individual response with your group, you'll get a better sense of what all the operative UGRs that connect to this particular lead-in sentence really are.

2. Next, be prepared to change your assumptions about what's working, what isn't, and what the right next steps might be. The whole point of this undertaking is change, and that means you must use the responses you read here to identify a path forward.

3. Before you even start worrying about what to do next (or whom to hold accountable for what you read), have a discussion together and reach consensus on the performance impact score. This is the real reason for your group being assembled. "Who said this?" is not the point of this meeting.

4. Bear in mind that each and every one of the responses you are about to read reflect someone's perceptions of the way we do things around here, and that these UGRs were the way that they are before we did this Stock Take. Doing the Stock Take did not create the UGRs, but doing the Stock Take gave us, for the first time, the capacity to understand them.

5. Finally, be patient with yourself and others in the days and weeks that follow. It took you a while to reach this point. You are not going to turn it all around overnight.

Helen put the sheet on the table. Dave drew a deep breath, looked Helen in the eye, and asked, "Okay, what do we do now?"

Helen sniffed and said, "Well, I guess we'd better get to work. Let's read all the completed responses. I've got a bit of an advantage, since I've reviewed all the responses already. But I think it would probably be a good idea for me to hear this batch again from beginning to end."

Helen handed Donna an envelope marked "COMMUNICATION," which she opened and read aloud. Here is some of what she read:

"Around here, when you need information to solve a problem..."

...timing is everything. Wait for the right time to approach the right people. (POSITIVE)

...it's available via our systems. (POSITIVE)

...some people are more than happy to help you. (POSITIVE)

...you may have a test of your self-sufficiency, as you would at other organisations. (NEUTRAL)

...you need to know the right people to go to. (NEUTRAL)

...you need to know where to look. (NEUTRAL)

...you are completely on your own—and you are up the creek without a paddle. (NEGATIVE)

...you had better have friends in the right places. (NEGATIVE)

...there is probably going to be some kind of a blame game when the problem goes unsolved, so cover your freaking tracks. (NEGATIVE)

...you are no longer in control. (NEGATIVE)

...you had better be ready for someone to start assigning blame for whatever problem it is that you discovered, and you had better be ready to jump out of the way when the fingers start to point in your direction. (NEGATIVE)

...you are sometimes better off pretending you did not even hear about the problem in the first place. (NEGATIVE)

...it's not what you know, it's who you know. (NEGATIVE)

...the problem is, very often, not going to get solved until it becomes a crisis. (NEGATIVE)

...you are dead if the problem is serious and it has your name on it, because everyone's got their own little fiefdom to run, and they don't care about you. (NEGATIVE)

...good luck, because you're on your own. (NEGATIVE)

...don't let some people know that you need this. (NEGATIVE)

Helen was looking at her hands again. She brought them to her temples and smoothed her hair. She closed her eyes.
"It's all true," she said.

Dave stared at the floor for an awkward moment, wondering whether Helen expected him to say something confrontational. Somehow, though, he didn't have the stomach for it.

Finally, Helen opened her eyes and said, "I have to tell you something, Dave. All day yesterday, I felt like I had to figure out whose fault all this was. This morning, I don't feel like that anymore."

"No? So how do you feel today?"

"Like crap. Like it's my fault. Like I've wasted a lot of my own time and energy and let a lot of people down by allowing UGRs like these to take over my company. Like I've wasted good people's talents. Yours, for instance. Like I've got to start all over again. Listen, I owe you an apology. I hired you because you were creative; but then I wouldn't let you speak your mind."

"Well, I think there are really only two scenarios for us to consider here," Dave said. "One where we're drowning, maybe already sinking, and the other where we're alive and swimming for the shore. I've always been the 'swimming for it' type. What do you say we see if we can make it to dry land?"

Helen nodded. Donna smiled. I smiled.

The team got to work.

XLI:

"THERE WERE THREE BASIC THEMES that emerged," Dave told the group of senior managers, standing bravely (I thought) in a spot that was smack in the middle of the conference room. His shoulders were back; his chest was thrust out; his feet were planted steadily and firmly and did not move. The team surrounded him and eyed him warily. My mind hit "rewind" and spun backward thirty or so years. From a distance, Dave looked, for all the world, like Helen - the Helen Hardcharger who had stood confidently in front of our very first group of prospective venture capitalists and pitched our ideas for this company, and, back then, made me proud to be on her team.

"The main themes for the positive responses," Dave said, without the benefit of written notes, "was that information is generally available, some people are happy to help you out if you have a problem to solve, and you can find solutions to problems if your timing is right.

"As far as the neutral responses go, the main theme here was 'It depends.' People in this category felt that you needed to know where to look if you had a problem on your hands, and you needed help tracking down the information necessary to solve it.

"And the theme for our most popular category, negative, was multi-tiered. There were three big common elements that showed up repeatedly: One, if you have a problem and need information, you are on your own. Two, if you have a problem and need information, you are not really in control of your own destiny. And three, if you have a problem, you had better be sure that your name isn't associated with it, because there are likely to be reprisals of some kind or another."

A little silence settled over the conference room, broken only by the shuffling of a few papers.

Dave Dude reached for a notebook and began scanning some notes he had jotted down.

"Our next job," Dave said, "was to figure out, on a scale of negative ten to positive ten, the real-world impact on our bottom line if everything we heard in those completed lead-in sentences was an accurate reflection of the culture and the UGRs around here. After some discussion, everyone in our group agreed that what we saw in those sentences was, in fact, reflective of the UGRs people are operating by in our company. And I think you should know that there was a good deal of disagreement about the right number to assign to all of this for our performance impact score."

Someone chuckled softly in the back of the room, apparently on the assumption that Helen was once again managing and packaging the company news.

"Can you clarify exactly what you mean by that?" The voice from the back of the room sounded like that of Clive Nitpicker, the VP of accounting. "What kinds of disagreements are we talking about, specifically?"

"Donna and I felt that the right number to assign here was a negative six. But Helen disagreed."

Another tiny chuckle, impossible to place at any one spot in the room, tumbled out, probably involuntarily.

"And what was the outcome there?" asked another voice. It could have been Clive's pal, Mildred Muckrake, the communications director. Its unspoken subtext was *As if we didn't know.*

"Ultimately, we decided to go with Helen's number—"

"Humph," said another voice that could have belonged to Mildred's best friend, Tess Talebearer, who was the second-in-command in communications.

"Because," Dave continued, "Helen made a very persuasive argument that, with ineffective team interactions and lousy problem solving - both caused by poor communication - the whole organisational paralysis problem is only going to get worse in the days and weeks to come. So, in the end, we all agreed on her number, which was a negative nine."

> Naysayers can sap energy from a room. This can be trying for everyone, but bear in mind that improving the culture requires that you allow everyone to vent in an appropriate way. Very often, simply being exposed to the company's current UGRs can inspire people to re-evaluate their own behaviours.

The chuckling stopped. I thanked the first team for their hard work and honesty, and we moved on to the next group.

VII
XLII:

VARIATIONS ON "AROUND HERE,..."

I N SUCCESSION, THE OTHER GROUPS made their reports. Their findings were enlightening.

Around here, customers are...

Positive: 56 percent. The key themes: "our number one priority," "treated well."
Neutral: 20 percent. The key theme: "depends how important a client they are."
Negative: 24 percent. The key themes: "treated like numbers," "an interruption to our working day."

Performance impact score: +2

Around here, people are treated...

Positive: 29 percent. The key themes: "Within our team, really well," "Generally with respect."
Neutral: 26 percent. The key themes: "It varies," "Sometimes they are treated well."

Negative: 45 percent. The key themes: "Like dirt," "As soon as things get difficult, really bad," "It depends on what level you're at."

Performance impact score: -6

Around here, when you come up with a new idea...

Positive: 21 percent. The key themes: "My boss recognises it," "Supervisor praises you."
Neutral: 19 percent. The key themes: "It depends on whether it will cost money or not," "Hard to say," "Within small teams, things are okay."
Negative: 60 percent. The key themes: "It disappears into a black hole," "They say they want ideas, but no one wants feedback," "It's not worth the effort unless you work for a small team."

Performance impact score: -6

Around here, when someone says he or she will do something...

Positive: 36 percent. The key themes: "It's usually carried out," "People try as hard as they can."
Neutral: 23 percent. The key theme: "Sometimes it gets done, sometimes not."
Negative: 41 percent. The key themes: "It depends on who asks to get it done," "Don't hold your breath; there's always a crisis," "You have to keep hounding them."

Performance impact score: -5

Around here, when it comes to dealing with other departments...

Positive: 15 percent. The key themes: "If you know the right people, things usually go well," "Two departments in particular are good to deal with: marketing and administration."
Neutral: 22 percent. The key themes: "It varies," "It depends on the day."
Negative: 63 percent. The key themes: "People are not interested," "People are always looking to apportion blame," "If it means extra work, they don't want to know about it."

Performance impact score: -7

XLIII: A WEIGHTY VOTE

"WHAT I WANT TO DO now," I explained to the chattering group in a loud, clear voice, "is take a vote."

A sudden silence fell over the room, as though things had instantly become quite serious. All the back-and-forth, all the tensely concealed curiosity, all the politicking pretending that it wasn't politicking, had evaporated. People were now staring at me with faces of implausible blankness. I knew pretty much what they were thinking, because I was thinking (I felt sure) the same thing: clearly, we were all about to decide something, and clearly Helen was taking part in the process.

What would, what could, possibly emerge from such a vote?

I pulled out the notes that I had hastily composed during my most recent phone call with Sam Sherlock, double-checked them to make sure what I was about to say was what I was supposed to say, and then replaced them in the breast pocket of my jacket.

"The way this works," I said to the hushed assembly, "is that everyone gets three votes, and we each cast our votes for the lead-in sentences that we feel most strongly should be worked on here, today, in order to support our own company. Each of us can allocate those three votes in whatever way we want, but however we decide to allocate them, the three sentences that receive the most votes will be the ones we will invest our time, energy, and attention in today and tomorrow. Here are the six sentences once again, accompanied by the performance impact scores each sub-group assigned to them.

"Remember, this is a weighted vote—you can give your three votes to one sentence or spread them across the board. Let's take a look at the options."

I wrote the sentences and the scores on the whiteboard:

"Around here, when you need information
to solve a problem..."   -9

"Around here, customers are..."   +2

"Around here, people are treated..."   -6

"Around here, when you come up
with a new idea..."   -6

"Around here, when someone says he or
she will do something..."   -5

"Around here, when it comes to dealing
with other departments..."   -7

"And in case you were wondering," I said, "no, this is not an anonymous vote. We are beyond the point, I think, where we need that. Each person will write their votes on the flip chart. Once the counting is done, we'll determine the top three sentences that we need to work on. Before you cast your vote, consider this question:

"Where would we get the most value for the company if we were able to measurably improve that particular aspect of our culture?"

"So please, before you do cast your vote, bear this in mind: at present we are talking only about implementing things that are both believable and doable.

"The three aspects of our culture that we choose to work on now shouldn't require some major process, or a million dollars, or a special gathering of all the members of the board of directors, in order to bear fruit. The votes that we cast right now should *only* be cast in order to generate positive, measurable results in the short term. So, if the only thing we can come up with in a given area is to launch some intricate, long-term campaign that will take a long time to pay off before anyone can see any of the positive impacts or notice any improvements in our bottom line, then that's not what we want to vote for.

"Okay. We are ready. Take a moment, talk among yourselves if you want to, and consider carefully how you want to cast your three votes."

I watched as they all stared at the list that I had written on the board. They were taking their task seriously, very seriously indeed. Just about every person in the room had an expression of careful, attentive thought, and no one appeared to be in a hurry to "vote and get it over with."

After a while, everyone had cast their vote. These were the three sentences the group (including Helen) decided to work on:

"Around here, when you need information
to solve a problem..."   -9

"Around here, when you come up
with a new idea..."   -6

"Around here, when it comes to dealing
with other departments..."   -7

For the record, Helen cast all three of her votes for "Around
here, when you need information to solve a problem..."

XLIV

XLIV:

JOINED HELEN, DAVE DUDE, DONNA Messwidme, and Clive Nitpicker in the little meeting room that now served as the impromptu home of the "TalkTime" subgroup, so named because it was dedicated to supporting the key cultural attribute of communication.

The five of us were to work together to come up with ideas for possible changes –changes that would support a new and different set of UGRs, a new way of working every day, in the area of communicating with each other. All the changes we came up with had to meet three simple criteria: they had to be implementable by everyone in the organisation; they had to be clearly related to helping us improve our bottom line; and they had to represent something we could do now, in the short term, without having to invest large amounts of time, money, or organisational attention to make the change happen.

"I want to start out," Helen said quietly, "by acknowledging that better communication starts with this meeting, and it starts with me. I want to make a promise to everyone in this room that what you say in here will stay in here. I also want to let you know that whatever you decide to share with the group today will never be held against you in any way or used to make your career here more difficult. Or shorter. We've got some problems here, and we've got to get to the bottom of them, I know. So, just to level with you, I really don't think we can expect to make any kind of headway on addressing those problems until you all feel that you can speak your mind here. So if you're worried about repercussions for telling me what you really think is happening around here, and specifically in my office, you can stop worrying. I want to hear what people are really thinking about this issue. I know you're all used to hearing me. And the only warning I have to give you is this one: I intend to give as good as I get here. So yes, I do want to hear what's on your minds. And yes, you should be ready to hear what I've got to say too."

That sobered the room up pretty quickly. The chitchat and light joshing that had kept the place in "transition mode" had evaporated, and it was now quite clear that it was time to get down to business.

> Before you embark on the task of fixing existing UGR-related problems, take another close look at the themes and patterns you and your team identified in the UGRs Stock Take. Ask: What is the underlying problem that connects these themes, what is its root cause, and what could we do about it right now, without allocating large amounts of time and money?

"Bruce, this is your meeting. Help us get started."

"Okay, Helen," I said. "Will do."

I made my way over to the whiteboard, wiped it clean, and wrote this question in big letters:

WHAT ARE THE MAJOR THEMES THAT WE SAW?

"I know we identified these themes for the rest of the team already," I said, "but I think it will help us set our priorities if we restart from this point. What do we know now? If we start from that question, we can move on to the question that it's our job to answer now, which is 'What can we conclude about what we know, and what should we do about it?' So let's get started. Who wants to recap the positive themes?"

"I can do that," said Dave, beaming and apparently eager to grab the opportunity to focus on something optimistic. "The positive theme sounded like this: When you've got a problem to solve, the information is out there. It's generally available, some people are happy to help you out, and if your timing is good, you can be part of some breakthroughs."

"How about the neutral themes?" I asked.

"Let me take that one," Donna said. "As far as the neutral responses go, the big theme was 'It depends.' You need to know where to look if you are facing a problem and you don't yet have the information you need to solve it."

"And who wants to recap the big themes that we saw as negatives, as obstacles to the UGRs we need to build into our company, starting now?"

"I will," said Helen. "They were: If you have a problem and need information, you are on your own. If you have a problem and need information, you are not really in control of your own destiny anymore. And if you have a problem, you had better be sure that your name isn't associated with it, because there are likely to be reprisals at some point."

"So now it's time to look at the million-dollar question: What's the cause of that negativity? Why were the negative responses so much more numerous than the positives and the neutrals? Where is all this coming from? Are there any lead-in sentences that jump out at anyone as being particularly important to use to begin the discussion?"

Clive Nitpicker pulled out his file folder and retrieved the lead-in sentences that the rest of us had reviewed at the previous meeting. I had made a copy for him, and he now scanned that copy as though it were the Rosetta stone.

"May I ask a procedural question, Bruce?" Clive said with the exquisite, overpolite politeness I had long associated with conversations with him.

"Of course."

"Does picking one of these sentences preclude us from coming back to look at other sentences later on in the discussion?"

"Absolutely not," I assured him.

"Good. I was hoping you'd say something like that," Clive said, smiling.

Clive then proposed that we look at this sentence to begin with—the very same one that had attracted my attention:

> Around here, when you need information to solve a problem you had better be ready for someone to start assigning blame for whatever problem it is that you discovered, and you had better have evidence ready when the fingers start to point in your direction. (NEGATIVE)

XLV: HELEN LISTENS FOR A CHANGE

"SO, WHAT DO YOU SUPPOSE that sentence says about our current UGRs, about how we agree to communicate?"

"Well," said Donna, having noticed that Helen was, for the moment, holding her tongue, "I suppose it says something about the daily importance of not being blamed for something going wrong. That seems to be a big priority for people. Not being the one whose fault it is."

All around the table, thoughtful heads nodded, including Helen's.

"I have to say," Dave Dude offered, "that this whole 'blame' thing was one of the big culture shocks I experienced when I came on board here. I was recruited in a pretty aggressive way, and I was told a lot of things about how the company worked. I felt it was a great opportunity to come here, because I agreed with the idea of constructive conflict, which was what Helen and everyone else said made the place tick: the principle of standing your ground and defending your ideas, the principle of putting your own skin in the game, the principle of mixing things up and learning from one another by challenging each other's ideas and identifying the weak spots in someone's argument so you could make the group's approach stronger. All of that was absolutely true—that really is how we make a lot of decisions here, and sometimes it's very constructive and very positive. But the other side of 'creative conflict' is blame. People have become wary of asking for help or seeking out the information they need, because they don't feel like going through a nuclear war in order to get the help or the information, and they don't feel like losing the nuclear war, either. I think in a lot of ways, what people told me about the 'creative conflict' we all experience here was incomplete. Sometimes it's creative. And sometimes it's a tactic for shifting the blame onto someone else."

We all took that in for a moment and processed it. There was a kind of relief in the air, intangible but very real, at the phenomenon of hearing someone say out loud something that had been on all our minds for so long. Perhaps part of the relief lay in the fact that Helen was, true to her word, refraining from judging, criticising, or attacking Dave for saying this to her face. Dave! Of all people!

"Okay. Where are we right now, as far as that blame game goes? How would you describe how that game operates in your world?" I asked. "Anybody?"

Clive tapped his pencil on his legal pad a few times, more and more rapidly, as though revving an unseen mental motor, and then cleared his throat.

"I would say," he announced, forming his words carefully and slowly, "that the game we are all currently best at playing in my department could best be summarised as 'The best defence is a good offense.' In other words, there are plenty of situations we all face, dozens of them each day, no doubt, where we decide that it is a much higher priority to make sure that someone outside of our department gets blamed for a problem than it is to make sure that the problems get solved. That's what I see. That's the game we play with other departments, because it's the game they play with us. I don't know who started it, or why, but it multiplied, and it's what's happening everywhere."

Everyone in the room seemed to take a deep breath, as though we were all eager to prove to ourselves that none of us was in a dream, that we were, in fact, speaking our minds on such things, with Helen in the room, and were, apparently, going to live to tell the tale.

"So what would you say are the root causes of us all playing that game?" Helen asked suddenly. "Where is it coming from? I'm not kidding. I want to hear it."

It was Dave who spoke first.

"Honestly, Helen, I think it comes from fear," he said. "I think fear is the ultimate root cause here. Fear of being blamed for something you didn't do. Fear of being blamed for something you *did* do. Fear of a project collapsing and a big client noticing. Fear of being the person left holding the bag. And let me be clear. I don't believe this fear is traceable to any one person. I believe it is just the way we have all silently agreed to interact with one another. And if any of us think this is all down to the way Helen runs meetings, I'm afraid that's an oversimplification we can't afford. It's the way we spread the fear down the chain that's killing this place."

We spent half an hour on that one. To her credit, Helen took careful notes on exactly what was working and what wasn't working in her meetings with senior staff. We concluded that Helen was sometimes impatient with the amount of time it took to create a meaningful consensus on complex issues. As a result, she sometimes issued edicts before each member of the senior management team felt he or she had been heard. This led to hard feelings and to a cycle of fear and recrimination—because poor decisions sometimes came back to haunt the very executives who had felt excluded from the decision-making process. Very often, Helen held her own direct reports accountable for "not speaking up" but then continued to make it difficult for them to speak up the next time around.

In addition, we concluded that:

- Many senior executives were not sharing information effectively with the members of their own teams. There were plenty of examples of leaders sharing information selectively for the purpose of making another department or other individuals look bad.

- All the senior executives were, from time to time, portraying decisions being made "at the top" as something that they had no responsibility for—often prefacing their words with the phrase "Helen says." "Helen says" meant that the speaker wanted to distance himself or herself from whatever followed. "Helen says" translated, loosely, as "I don't expect this decision to work, and I won't be the source of any criticism or consequences if you ignore or sabotage this decision." When executives used the words "Helen says," they were sending the signal that they were no longer stakeholders, and they were protesting the fact that they felt they had no input in, and no impact on, major decisions.

> A common symptom of communication-related UGRs that do not support the organisation is the phrase "Jim says" (where "Jim" equals "someone higher in the command chain than I am" and "says" equals "this is not what I would say or will support").

XLVI.

"**I**T IS TIME," SAM SHERLOCK told me over the phone that night, "for a bit of old-fashioned leadership."

"What does that mean?" I asked.

"Well, Bruce, you've finally gotten through to the leadership team and gotten them on board, for which I think you probably deserve a Nobel Peace Prize. But I'm afraid that's not enough. Now it's time to put those leaders to work and move forward. Tomorrow morning, I want you to turn each and every one of the senior leaders you've been working with thus far into an evangelist."

> In the "Teach" step, we familiarise as many people as possible within the organisation with the UGRs concept. This requires a process of evangelisation.

"An evangelist?"

"If you open your dictionary and go to the end of the *E* section, you will find a whole lot of different definitions for the word 'evangelist,'" he explained. "My favourite one sounds like this: 'a zealous advocate of a cause.' You've now got a whole lot of people working at the Very Important Corporation, and so far, only eighteen of them—the members of your management team—have any clear idea of what a UGR is. That means that any attempt to paste this

123

onto the rest of the company will be seen as just another 'flavour of the week' project, something that will go away if enough people ignore it for long enough."

"So how do we avoid that?" I asked.

"Simple," he said matter-of-factly. "You convince the senior management team to carry the gospel—as it were—to all the places where it was previously unknown. That's how you're going to earn your pay."

XLVII
CULTURE CLUB

FOLLOWING THE ADVANCES THAT WE'D made with the team during the recently completed two-day work session, Helen and I decided that we needed to keep the momentum going – and we agreed to schedule a follow-up session with the management team as soon as possible. It was good to agree on something important for a change, and reminded me of how we did things in the early days.

Looking over the results of the Stock Take analysis that we'd completed at the precious session, we also came to the realisation – the very one that Sam had shared with me one-on-one. What we needed now was a way to engage everyone in the company in the same principles we had learned together with the management team. Otherwise, we ran the risk of the whole process being seen as some new piece of vacuous management-speak.

When rolling out the company-wide UGRs program, it is best to do so face-to-face, in person. In some situations, video previews and reinforcements can also be helpful.

We agreed to roll out the UGRs process across the company.

"Okay, Bruce," Helen said, smiling. "You're the driver here. How do we do this?"

"What I propose now," I told her, "is a concentrated series of face-to-face all-company meetings. These meetings should play out over the course of a week or two. They should be preceded by a short video that we in the executive team put together, a video that prepares everyone in the organisation for the change in thinking they're about to experience. That change didn't come instantly to us, and I don't think we should assume it will come instantly to them."

"Fine," said Helen. "Set up the timing for these meetings, clear it with Donna, and tell me what you need from me. Let's gather the troops."

XLVIII

VIDEO, VIDEO

I
N OUR INITIAL ALL-COMPANY MEETINGS, which involved both mid-level leaders and other staff (who we called 'Champions') as organising forces, we covered the first three steps of the process. Specifically, we made sure everyone was aware of the three KCAs that we had identified as particularly important:

- Open communication at all times
- Displaying initiative and innovation at all times
- Respect for people across all boundaries

This was the "Envision" step.

We also went through the results of the UGRs Stock Take with them, and we asked everyone for their views on improvement actions that might be taken. Sam had made a special point of telling me how important it was for management to bring everyone in the organisation up-to-date on the Stock Take results and all the work

It's extremely important that managers respect, re-cord, and report the feed-back arising from discus-sions about the Stock Take. Always be on the lookout for new "hot spots" that have not yet entered the discussion.

connected to it, and then to ask directly for feedback and ideas for improvement. All of this was a part of the "Assess" step.

At the end of the day, we held both all-team and small-group discussions about UGRs and the specifics of how they drive people's behaviour. This was the "Teach" step.

As part of the Teach step, we also shared a short, upbeat video describing all the steps we had gone through thus far. In the video, Helen and all the other members of the senior management team (including me) shared our own personal views on the power of UGRs. This turned out to be a very powerful teaching tool. Making the video helped reinforce what we ourselves had learned, and it gave us a few new insights, as well!

At the end of the day, we had gathered a lot of good feedback on the realistic, practical things that could be done to make improvements in the areas of concern identified in our Stock Take.

The "Teach" step is all about teaching people about UGRs and their power and demonstrating how an individual's own personal behaviour connects with UGRs.

This face-to-face approach not only guaranteed that we got important ideas and suggestions from the front line, but it also proved that, around here, you could talk about UGRs out loud on a Monday morning and still have a job on Monday afternoon. That, in and of itself, was a powerful teaching tool and a major step forward in building a culture that actually supported our end game.

XLVIX
REVIEW TIME

THE SENIOR LEADERSHIP TEAM THEN reviewed the outcomes from the all-team meetings.

We looked at all the notes, shared our own impressions, and talked everything over. It took us about an hour to come to a consensus about the best actions for us to take in response to what we'd heard. The actions we agreed to follow through on fell into three categories:

- **Personal style commitments.** For instance, Clive Nitpicker made this commitment to the group: "As a leader, I'm going to go out of my way to listen more carefully to my people's concerns." His accountability on that point was now a matter of record within our management group.

- **System commitments.** For instance, Helen made this commitment: "We're going to ensure we have a company-wide communiqué that goes out every two weeks. It's going to update everyone on important events and analyse the latest news from a UGRs perspective."

- **Special initiatives.** For instance, when two depart-ments—in this meeting's case, accounting and sales—have the obligation to work closely together on an upcoming project, we organise a meeting where each department asks the other, "How can we help you do your job better?"

Ensure that people see and experience *personal style commitments, system* commitments, and *special initiatives* as being direct consequences of the UGRs Stock Take and the staff feedback from the session.

Importantly, all these improve-ment initiatives were branded, both within our group and outside of it, as being a consequence of the UGRs pro-cess and the staff feedback from the sessions. Almost immediately, people at all levels of our organisation began to see things happening as a direct consequence of their input.

THE ART OF INVOLVEMENT:

BY THE TIME THE SECOND round of all-company meetings rolled around, the whole company was buzzing. Every single department, every single team, every single employee had ideas and feedback to share.

During this second round of staff meetings, we made a point of engaging our people in the activity of creating new, positive, aspirational UGRs—UGRs that linked to the KCAs we'd identified as critical to the company's survival. We asked, "If those KCAs were alive and well around here, what would some of the UGRs be?" This was the "Involve" step.

By the time we were finished with this second round of meetings, each member of the executive team had dozens of suggestions to record and collate and, of course, attribute to individual team members.

> The "Involve" step is a company-wide discussion that begins with the assumption that people can affect their own working culture.

Under the subject line "A good sign?" I e-mailed my own team's input to Sam Sherlock the day before our big debriefing meeting with Helen. It was night for me, but six o'clock in the morning for Sam, thanks to the time difference between Sydney and New York City.

"This is not a good sign," Sam said over the phone, a little groggy but sounding excited.

"It's not?"

"No. This is a *great* sign."

"How so?" I asked.

"The 'Involve' step that you have just completed is a really important step, Bruce. It's the step that prevents this from becoming another slogan, another poster, another forgettable campaign. It's the step that builds on the previous steps by engaging people in creating, then prioritising positive, aspirational UGRs by which they would like to characterise the company into the future. It's the step where we get people to complete the sentence 'Around here,...' framing it as though it already exists. These, of course, should be linked to the KCAs. I can reassure you that this is completely safe territory for leaders—as people will come up with positive UGRs that leaders cannot disagree with. And remember, this isn't a rulebook. It's a conversation. You and Helen are on your own now. You're the ones who have got to

> When creating new, positive UGRs, frame them as though the critical KCA you have identified already exists. Think about what it would be like to work in an environment where that KCA is already alive and well. What would people already be doing? What would the positive UGR be that would prove the team was already operating in full alignment with that KCA? Also—a tip for creating positive UGRs is to think about something that is happening now that you don't like and flip it around to the positive.

navigate that conversation within the company, if you want any of this to stick, that is."

There was silence on the line as I pondered that for a moment.

"I'm going back to bed," Sam said, "but do let me know how it goes."

In the "Involve" step, you engage people in creating and prioritising aspirational, positive UGRs—linked to the KCAs—by which they would like to characterise the organisation into the future. The outcomes will feed into the next step, "Embed."

ACCENTUATE THE POSITIVE

SHORTLY AFTER I HUNG UP with Sam, Helen called and asked me whether I would synthesise all the information that had been submitted from all the different work groups and lead the meeting with the senior managers the next morning. I was more than happy to take on both tasks.

When it comes to building positive UGRs, the process really is more important than the content. In other words, you can change the words as long as you've got the involvement of people in the organisation, but you can't take away the involvement and expect nice-sounding words to accomplish anything.

"The first piece of good news," I told the assembled group of senior managers bright and early the next morning, "is that just about everyone at the Very Important Corporation is now involved with this process. That's much more significant than any of the wording we may come up with here, because the process is actually more important than the content."

"The second piece of good news," I continued, "is that, without any prompting from us, the company as a whole strongly supports the three KCAs that we chose as our top priorities. Those are, as you may recall..."

And I wrote the three relevant KCAs once again on the whiteboard:

- Open communication at all times
- Displaying initiative and innovation at all times
- Respect for people across all boundaries

"From this point forward," I said, "each one of us now faces a major challenge as managers.

"As you know, we're about to look at, and continue, the 'Involve' step. Well, in order to generate good draft ideas from our teams about what the positive UGRs should sound like in each of those three areas, we all had to do two things: we had to promise our people they could speak their minds without fear of retribution, and we had to listen carefully to what we heard when they did speak.

"Well, we did that.

"Now, I know we did it, because there's no way we could have generated the responses that I saw from our own people if we hadn't. But now we each have to acknowledge that we've got a responsibility. We've opened the door and let the daylight shine on

Once people are finally taking part in the discussion that creates new UGRs that will support the organisation and move it forward, you have a sense of ownership, a sense of being a stakeholder, that is not otherwise there. This new sense of ownership amounts to a contract between management and the front line that the "old days" are over and that speaking up, in appropriate ways, will now result in positive change for everyone.

some major internal problems. If, at this stage, we decide to shut that door, we are in serious trouble. If we ever give our people evidence that we've stopped listening, if we ever make them wonder if we really were acting in good faith, if we ever get complacent and stop following through and addressing the problems we've identified, if we ever slip back into a cycle of recrimination then we will only have made our situation worse. My point is, we are off to a good start, but keeping this dialogue alive is not Helen's job alone. It's ours."

Helen, who had already seen my summary of the results, asked, "Bruce, the only way they're going to be able to do that is by asking good questions. In your view, what's the single most important question that we're now asking people during the 'Involve' stage? I ask because I want to make sure that we keep on asking it as we go forward."

"If I had only one question that I could ask someone at this stage," I said, "it would sound like this: What is something that you don't like, and what would it sound like if you flipped it around to something you would like and then started it with the words 'Around here,'?"

> When creating positive UGRs, think about something you don't like, and then flip it around to a positive.

Helen smiled a little and looked at Dave Dude, who smiled back. "Go on," Helen said. "Give us an example of how that works."

"Well, one of the people who reports to me is a data analyst named Melanie Middle-Ground," I said. "She's someone I would describe as a straight shooter, a solid performer, and an extremely supportive person, both in the workplace and outside of it. When we were talking about the communication attribute, Melanie told me, 'Bruce, I just don't like the amount of negative gossip, all the backbiting that happens in our company.'

"So I said, 'Okay, tell me what that would sound like if it were a UGR that was flipped around. If that new, positive ground rule started with the words 'Around here,' what would it be?'"

"She thought for a moment, and then she said, 'Around here, people are approached directly and constructively when there's a problem.'"

"So that's what I wrote down. In fact, it was one of the best responses I got."

Everyone nodded in agreement. Helen did too. Apparently, they all liked Melanie's positive UGR.

"And so, if I understand you right," Dave Dude said, "what you're about to share with us are the most helpful of the positive UGRs that we've gathered so far—from the front lines of every department in the company?"

"That's it," I said. "These are the most relevant of the new, positive ground rules that our own team members came up with for these three KCAs."

"Bring them on," said Dave Dude.

HELEN GETS THE LAST WORD AFTER ALL

"**T**HE FIRST OF OUR THREE most important key cultural attributes," I told our senior managers, "has to do with communication. You all remember it, I think:

- Open communication at all times

"Fortunately for us, the members of our team not only agreed that this was our single most important KCA, they also gave us dozens of positive, constructive ways to finish that sentence. Here are the UGRs they offered that seemed the most powerful and relevant to me."

I flicked on the projector and screened the first slide:

- Around here, people know where to go when they need information.
- Around here, people are supported and praised for explaining what they need and why they need it.
- Around here, people get the information they need to solve problems.

- Around here, people solve problems together and share the credit.
- Around here, everyone can become part of the solution.
- Around here, people are approached directly and constructively when there's a problem.
- Around here, when we have a problem, we talk about it with the people who can fix it.
- Around here, when you say you don't know something, you're never penalised or put down for that.
- Around here, you can discuss problems openly without being penalised.

"The next KCA was:

- Displaying initiative and innovation at all times

"Here again, we came up with a wealth of great responses from our frontline employees. Here are the six that seemed, to me, to be the most compelling:

As you begin the process of formulating new, positive UGRs, use the KCAs as starting points, then keep writing down all the positive UGRs you can, whether or not they match up with the ideas you began with.

- Around here, you get a fair hearing.
- Around here, you know you can share new ideas openly, without fear of any negative consequences.
- Around here, people acknowledge you for taking the initiative with a creative solution, whether or not it is implemented.

- Around here, you begin with collaboration.
- Around here, you get credit both personally and as a member of the team when you have a good idea.
- Around here, everyone supports you, regardless of whether or not they think your idea is a good one.
- Around here, we are open to new ways of doing things.

"The last of our three high-priority KCAs was:

- Respect for people across all boundaries

"Here are the most persuasive complete sentences I saw that addressed this attribute:

- Around here, we make an honest effort to understand what people on the other team have to deal with.
- Around here, we are frank and honest with each other.
- Around here, we listen first.
- Around here, we begin from the assumption that there is a win-win outcome waiting to be found.
- Around here, we think about the end-result impact on our external customers.
- Around here, we recognise that everything we do is interconnected.
- Around here, we remind ourselves and others to treat everyone with respect.

"Wow," said Dave Dude. "I think that last idea sums up everything we've been working toward, in all six of the attributes."

I glanced around the room quickly, met someone's gaze, and then turned back to Dave. "Twelve words that say it all," I said, "but look how long it took us to find those twelve words and how hard we had to work to align our organisation with them."

"Who came up with that sentence?" Dave asked.

"I'm not sure I'm supposed to say," I answered.

"Aw, come on," Clive Nitpicker objected. "You can tell us. It's a great contribution. We ought to know who made it."

There was an awkward silence. I shut off the projector.

"Bruce," said Donna Messwidme, "you aren't getting off that easily. Tell us who gave you that ground rule."

"That one was mine," Helen Hardcharger said finally.

TIGHTENING IT UP:

"**W**HAT WE ARE AFTER HERE**,**" Helen told us after a coffee break, "is a distillation of the most useful UGRs we've seen. We may see the opportunity for some light revision, but we don't want major changes to what we've got in front of us now. What we are looking for is something that could fit onto an index card, or maybe even the back of a business card. We want to finalise a list of between three and six ground rules that everyone in the organisation can recognise as part of what they just worked on and remember with little or no effort. That means we have to make sure they are short."

Keep your positive UGRS short! Make sure they are written in real-world terms that everyone can understand. If any of your UGRs sound like a long-winded memo or a boring policy manual, revise them until they are crisp, direct, and accessible.

I was struck by how often Helen now used the word "we" as opposed to "I." Even though she had not even begun the fifth step of the process, it was obvious that her view of the company—and perhaps even her view of herself—had changed somehow because of all the work she had done over the past weeks. Yes, she had been working on the UGRs, but she had also been working on herself. It occurred to me that it was probably impossible for anyone to make progress in one area without making progress in the other.

> Working productively on your UGRS usually means working on yourself.

After an hour of collaboration, inspired horse-trading, and brainstorming, we came up with the following list:

- Around here, when you need information, people point you in the right direction.
- Around here, people are approached directly and constructively when there's a problem.
- Around here, we are open to new ways of doing things.
- Around here, we try to understand what people on the other team have to deal with.
- Around here, we are frank and honest with each other.
- Around here, we treat everyone with respect.

It all fit, as requested, on an index card. We were ready for the fifth step. But first, it was time for a celebration.

LIV: PARTY ON

BEFORE THAT WEEK WAS OUT, every department in every corner of the Very Important Corporation threw an impromptu multi-departmental UGRs party. This idea came from Helen herself, who sent out a brief personalised video invitation to everyone in the organisation.

The parties started that Friday at 4:00 p.m. sharp. Friends and loved ones were invited. On the walls, and in what seemed like every cubicle, were the UGRs we had sweated over, drafted, revised, and finalised together, as an organisation—in big type, little type, and in-between type. You couldn't possibly miss them. There were also colourful, handcrafted posters everywhere.

> Celebrate the official launch the positive UGRs that the company will be following. Make sure the launch is fun!

It certainly was not the first time we had plastered posters all over the place. But there was something different about this set of posters. Unlike previous "motivational" posters we had unleashed on the workforce—with single words like "excellence" set below an image of, say, a soaring hawk surveying its hunting terrain—these additions to our workspace did not inspire rude jokes, graffiti, or any other evidence of a division between "us" in management and "them" everywhere else. No matter which part of the company I visited (and I made a point of checking out a whole lot of our offices that week), people seemed to be *reading* these posters, nodding their heads as they said the words quietly, and even, wonder of wonders, discussing them with each other, right out loud. It was because they had actually had a voice in creating these posters, I surmised.

The UGR parties only accelerated that process. People relaxed and had fun with the whole concept of our "Unwritten Ground Rules." We celebrated the work we had done. And somehow, it wasn't just Helen and me and the rest of the executive team who were saying, "This is the line in the sand; this is the way we will work around here from now on; this is the day things change." It was all of us.

LV

THE BIGGEST CALL OF ALL COLLAPSES

"**T**HE TRICKY THING ABOUT THE fifth step, 'Embed,'" Sam told me over a finicky Skype connection that we had spent a frustrating quarter of an hour establishing, "and the part that people are the most likely to forget, is that..."

Then static. Absolutely incomprehensible.

"The part people are most likely to forget is what, Sam?"

More static.

"Now, you be sure you pass that part along to Helen and the rest of the team."

"Um...could you please repeat that, Sam?" I said. "I think I might have missed it."

> The fifth step, "Embed," is where you identify and implement strategies to embed the aspirational, positive UGRs.

"Sure," he said, upbeat and bouncy from somewhere far across the Internet. "I said, a lot of people make the mistake of thinking of the fifth step, 'Embed,' as"—static— "when in fact"—static— "we have to"—static— "Does that make sense?"

"I wish I could say it did, Sam," I answered mournfully. "You're dropping out. Quite a lot. Perhaps we should try this call on a standard telephone line?"

"No can do, Bruce," he said. "I'm headed for the Catalina Islands with the missus for a couple of weeks, and I've only got about thirty seconds before they make me turn off my iPad. Tell you what. Check your e-mail for"—static—"okay? I'll send it right now. Got to go."

"Sam? Sam?"

The Skype display read, "Call completed."

My hands and chest suddenly went numb. Panicked, I logged on to my e-mail account.

There was nothing from Sam.

It would be a long and strange week, a painful and largely improvisatory week, perhaps even a disastrous week, a week leading to the undoing of all that we had accomplished, if I got no guidance at all from Sam on how we were supposed to implement step five. I was on my own.

I kept checking my watch. Three minutes went by. Then five. Then ten. And still not a word from Sam via e-mail.

Finally, eleven minutes after our call tanked, I got the following message:

Two non-negotiable strategies for successfully embedding your positive UGRs:

- Make your positive UGRs visible to everyone, in both words and deeds.

- Incorporate UGRs as a standing agenda item in team meetings. These UGRs discussions should take place every two to three weeks and should focus for five minutes or more on "how we're doing" with respect to the positive UGRs.

Each of these elements is important but insufficient on its own. You need both.

To: Bruce
Fr: Sam

EMBED

Not the end, only the beginning

Visible

UGRs must be weekly agenda item up and down org

Ongoing dialog, clear rewards/consequences

NOT THE END

W ITH HELEN'S INPUT, I WROTE and sent an e-mail message to every member of the senior management team. Its heading was "STEP FIVE: EMBED. MUST READ."

Here is what it said:

Hi all—

The tricky thing about the fifth step of the UGRs process, "Embed," and the part that we senior managers are most likely to forget, is that it is not the end of anything.

Even though this is the fifth of the five steps, we must constantly remember, as we begin to implement all this within our enterprise, is that "Embed" **is not** the **final** step.

It's not the culmination of anything.

It's not the part where we get to sit back, relax, and watch what happens.

In fact, it's the **beginning** of the phase where we and other managers have to work the hardest.

Beginning this week, and continuing **forever**, each of us has the responsibility of ensuring that UGRs are a standing biweekly agenda item at team meetings taking place in any area of the company.

There are no exceptions to this. Each and every biweekly team meeting should include a short group discussion of what we all experienced over the past fourteen days and how our own choices and behaviours either did or did not align with the UGRs that we have agreed to operate by as an organisation.

It's likely to be an interesting series of meetings. We want to make sure everyone on the management team is in a position to learn from everything that takes place during this period.

As we begin to use and become more familiar with this process, it's particularly important for us to make sure there are no perceived penalties or recriminations for learning what it feels like to operate within a workplace that is guided by the UGRs we are all learning and implementing.

There will come a point at which there will be clear consequences for patterns of performance that run counter to our UGRs. But we have to learn what it is like to work this way before we learn what it is like to be penalised for not working this way.

In these critical first sixty to ninety days, as we begin learning how to ride this particular bicycle, please make sure you spend more time praising people for pedalling and keeping their balance than you do criticising them for falling down.

DO THIS: be sure to forward all relevant notes of all your UGR discussions to me via e-mail so that I can share them with Helen and the rest of the senior team.

The "Embed" process is not the end of anything. It is the beginning of a permanent cultural evaluation process.

Many thanks!

Bruce Bottomline

LVII
SUCCESS STORIES

EVENTUALLY, HELEN ASKED ME TO collect some of our "best practices"—which I took to mean our success stories—when it came to implementing the critical fifth step, "Embed." What follows in the next chapters are a few of those reports from the front lines (as it were) about how we managed to complete the critical "Embed" step at the Very Important Corporation. Of course, over the first few weeks and months of the "Embed" step, we made a point of noticing what worked, and we also made a point of celebrating internally whenever this happened. It wouldn't have made sense to do it the other way around: to make a big deal out of every obstacle we ran into or to throw the spotlight on people who were having trouble catching up with what we were doing.

Yet, as I assembled our "best practices," I realised that the great danger in reading these accounts (and, for that matter, in writing them) was that, when you encounter them in sequence, they may make the "Embed" process seem a little too magical, a little too easy, a little too smooth. In reality, there were many bumps along the way and many opportunities to remind ourselves that success lies not in the ability to avoid bumps in the road but in the ability to keep moving in the right direction.

I was surprised at how large a role humour played in the embedding of our positive UGRs. Most of the successful stories we assembled over those first sixty days—stories that played an invaluable role in helping us make the transition from "the kind of company we want to be" to "the kind of company we are" incorporated elements of fun and humour.

For instance, operations and sales had had a long history of run-ins concerning various reporting issues. A kind of back-and-forth rivalry had settled in, and despite my best efforts to stop it, nothing had seemed to work. In order to fit in as a "real" member of the accounting team, you had to magnify each perceived error of the sales department and tell the story of how some member of the sales team had neglected to file a report, or forgotten to fill in some essential part of a contract, or ignored a sign-off necessary to change standard specifications. In order to fit in as a member of the sales team, you had to gather evidence to support the narrative of an accounting department that was out to get you anyway and so might as well be ignored.

> Celebrate your own "best practices" and "success stories"—and use them as teaching tools—but don't imagine that you will be able to embed positive UGRs overnight. You won't. There will be challenges along the way that require patience, creativity, and persistence. Remember that this is a process, and it plays out in both the short and the long term.

During our weekly meeting of the leading accounting people, I heard the customary gripes about how horrific the salespeople were, and all I had to say was one word: "Whoops!"

At that, the whole team fell to silence, and the most experienced accountant in the room, Bob Beancounter, said, "I guess we forgot for a moment that we all understand what it is they have to deal with."

The room erupted in laughter, and we were able to move on without any further backbiting. (I got word from a colleague that almost exactly the same exchange took place on the sales side during the first week of our UGR rollout. But more on that later.)

Here's another success story. A long-standing Very Important Corporation tradition—but one more honoured, I always believed, in the breach than in the observance—was the "meeting before the meeting." This was a time-honoured tactic by which various cabals formed before "official" meetings in order to create strategies for distraction, delay, denial, or, if all else failed, delegation of responsibility to some other team or department. A parallel tradition, equally difficult to dislodge, was the "meeting after the meeting," where members of various secret and not-so-secret constituencies created strategies for undermining agreements they had just made with others in the company. Both practices stopped almost immediately after Helen sent the following leaflet to every employee via first-class mail:

***

"MEETINGS BEFORE THE MEETING"

AND "MEETINGS AFTER THE MEETING"

LEAD ONLY TO MORE FREAKING MEETINGS!

Save yourself! Save others! Work it out on the spot!

AROUND HERE, WE ARE FRANK AND HONEST WITH EACH OTHER.

AROUND HERE, PEOPLE ARE APPROACHED DIRECTLY AND CONSTRUCTIVELY WHEN THERE'S A PROBLEM!

***

(Note: As to the rumour that Helen herself once tried to launch a "meeting before a meeting" and was met with a smile and a leaflet from a senior manager, I have absolutely no comment on that.)

Another situation where humour carried the day was the solution to the "happy talk" challenge.

The issue here was a simple one. People would come up with new ways of approaching a challenge or problem but would face resistance, either overt or subtle, in gaining a larger audience within the company to evaluate, and perhaps even implement, the idea. The overt version of this brand of pre-emptive dismissal resembled Helen's now-infamous "Be careful, young man" remark to Dave Dude. That was clearly hostile and more than a little intimidating.

The subtle version, considerably more difficult to spot, took the form of warm praise followed by a manager's encouraging but meaningless promises to "consider" the idea being put forward and "perhaps" involve others in the organisation in the discussion. The manager was usually smiling broadly in this scenario, hence the name "happy talk." In both scenarios, we found (thanks to the standing UGRs agenda item in everyone's meetings) people were fast-forwarded past good ideas and missing opportunities for improvement.

Helen solved this problem by supplying everyone in the organisation with "DON'T BE CAREFUL" cards, which worked more or less like "Get Out of Jail Free" cards in Monopoly. The back of the card read, "AROUND HERE, WE ARE OPEN TO NEW IDEAS."

Any employee, in any part of the organisation, could "play" one of these cards once a week and, having done so, could share his or her idea with anyone in the organisation in the event that the person's manager did not sign on or suggest a plan of action. The cards were a huge success, because they immediately generated a big laugh whenever they were presented.

And once managers started laughing, they started listening.

LVIII:
BANANA AVERSION

As I said, though, there were many, many bumps in the road along the way, and it really wouldn't be fair to describe the process by which we embedded positive UGRs as just a series of success stories. There were plenty of failure stories along the way, and we learned from them as well. Here's one of them.

I hope you remember Milt Smooth, our company's VP of sales. He's the one who was admitted to the hospital with heart trouble on that awful day when I was trying to get out the door and catch my flight to Hawaii. About two months after that grim day, Milt, who had been with the company since the beginning, completed his recovery and decided to rejoin the company—on the strength of my promise to him, to his doctor, and to his wife that things were finally changing for the better at the Very Important Corporation.

Milt was an enthusiastic supporter of the process, and he was one of the biggest reasons that we were able to make some headway in calming the long-running rivalry between sales and accounting. While I was saying, "Whoops!" to the accounting people, Milt was usually saying, "Whoops!" to the people on the sales side. One of Milt's sales managers, Ted Toughtalk, was a veteran who had pretty much built his career, and his outlook on life, around the job of keeping that destructive accounting-versus-sales rivalry alive. Complicating matters was the fact that his team routinely beat its sales quotas.

At a time when every other manager who reported to Milt was carefully tamping out the fires, Ted was waiting with a box of matches and a bottle of kerosene, looking for the next chance to set a blaze while no one was looking. No amount of private discussion between him and Milt seemed to change things. The two had at least five documented one-on-one meetings, and promises to change were always made in those meetings, but the animosity kept flowing, as though Ted had never even heard a word of what he had discussed with Milt.

One day, I even overheard Ted telling a new hire in the employee lounge to remember that "Accounting is out to get you, and this whole Unwritten Ground Rules game that the company is playing is nothing but a big camouflage act that's meant to conceal that."

At that, he turned and reached for a coffee cup and saw me. Before I could say a word, he darted out of the room, leaving his cup and the baffled new sales hire far behind.

"I am afraid that what we have here," Sam told me during a phone call while discussing Ted's situation, "is a monkey who just plain hates bananas and wants to keep on hating bananas."

LVIX: JACK WELCH WEIGHS IN

"**M**AYBE YOU'VE HEARD OF A guy named Jack Welch," Sam said, his voice crystal clear—finally—over a landline.

"Sure," I replied.

"Welch had a saying at GE," Sam continued. "'Great cultures deliver great numbers. Great numbers don't deliver great cultures.' What he meant was that any truly effective leader needs to make personnel decisions that put workplace culture in the driver's seat. He did that by placing his own people into four quadrants. Check your e-mail. I just sent the quadrants to you."

Here's what I saw in the diagram I pulled up from my e-mail:

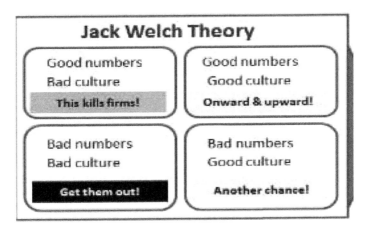

"This is a balancing act, and a lot of people say that even Welch couldn't manage it. But it's worth understanding. Obviously, you want to hold on tight to the 'Good Culture / Good Numbers' people. And just as obviously, you want to part company with the people who consistently land in the 'Bad Culture / Bad Numbers' category. The challenge comes with the people who habitually show up in the other two categories. We always take a risk when we hold on to people who are good for the culture but whose metrics are lousy. And, concerning what matters most to you right now, we also take a risk when we hold on to someone who is performing well on the numbers while detracting from the culture—the 'Bad Culture / Good Numbers' people. Your task, and Milt's, is to figure out whether that risk is worth taking here. I can't answer that for you, but I can tell you it's something you probably want to review closely with Helen. My instinct would be to let him go."

> The ability to support a positive workplace culture and act in accordance with positive UGRs must figure into your personnel decisions. But it's important to remember that this is an ongoing balancing act, one that is not going to be easy.

LX: TED GOES OFF THE BANANA FARM

MILT AND I SCHEDULED A joint performance assessment session with Ted Toughtalk. From the opening moments of the meeting, it was obvious that he was startled to see me and more than a little uncomfortable.

"Ted," I said, "I'll be straight with you. Your team's numbers are stellar. We need them. And we need you. The numbers are not why I'm here. I'm here with Milt today because Helen asked me to be here. And the reason Helen asked me to be here, Ted, is that the three of us have a problem. Up and down, as an organisation, we've worked hard to build and support the operating principle that we respect other departments and understand what they've got to go through. But Helen feels, as do Milt and I, that that ground rule hasn't yet gotten any real traction in your department. Is that assessment off base, or do you think we're right about that?"

Ted Toughtalk cleared his throat and shifted in his seat. "It's hard to say," he said finally. "Lots of people remember lots of different issues when it comes to dealing with accounting. For my part, I say live and let live. That's how I operate, and that's how I want my people to operate."

"Really?" Milt asked.

"Of course," Ted Toughtalk answered, his gaze steady and his breathing controlled.

We put Ted on notice that he had thirty days to clean up his act and stop bad-mouthing the UGRs about interdepartmental cooperation and respect.

Thirty days came and went without incident. On day thirty-one, Ted was overheard telling his team during a meeting that his "probation" had ended and that "the jerks in accounting" were now "fair game." He asked the fourteen salespeople who reported to him to submit expense reports laden with (intentional) errors so as to "even the score" with whoever had "busted" him.

> Behaviour that clearly violates and undermines positive UGRs should generate discussion and action.

Not one, not two, not three, but *four* different salespeople who heard all this alerted Milt via e-mail, who alerted me, so I could alert Helen.

Ten minutes after I hit "send," I got an e-mail message from Helen: "Let him go. He obviously can't stand a good banana, and he doesn't want to see anyone else eating one, either."

Ted left us the very next day. And that was the end of the toxic relationship between Sales and Marketing that had once been such a thorn in our side.

LVI

POLLY SIGNS ON

MILT AND I HAD CONDUCTED multiple interviews with Polly Proactive, the sales manager who ended up replacing Ted. She had sailed through the interview process with flying colours. She boasted a perfect résumé, and she seemed like a great match with our company. But I wanted to be sure. At the end of her first day on the job, I stopped by to check in with her and ask her what her impressions of the Very Important Corporation were.

She smiled and said, "I love this place. Even after only one day, I can tell the people here are really committed to supporting each other and communicating respectfully with each other. People listen to you and work with you to solve problems. And they support you when you come up with new ideas. Actually, it's exactly the kind of place I was hoping to find as my next employer."

She was only momentarily puzzled by the fist pump and the loud "Yes!" shout I gave upon hearing these words, but she dutifully returned the salute.

"*Yes!*" said Polly Proactive as she smiled and pumped her fist in the air.

What she didn't know was that we'd done it!

And here's one thing I learned: a new employee is the best test for the UGRs in a workplace. They see and feel the prevailing

UGRs during their first weeks on the job – and Polly witnessed everything we'd worked so hard to create.

I knew at the point that the posters could have come down. We'd changed our workplace culture.

LXII

"**Y**OU WANTED TO SEE ME, Helen?"

"Have a seat," Helen said, gesturing to a nearby chair. "We've just gotten the results of our most recent workplace culture check-up."

She was referring to our regular and ongoing re-evaluation of where we were in terms of our workplace culture.

We were using two major tools to do this – one being the UGRs Stock Take, the other being a 360 degree behavioural assessment, which measured the extent to which our leaders were demonstrating behaviours consistent with our KCAs.

"I've got good news and bad news. Which do you want to hear first?"

I stared at her warily. "Which do you think I should hear first?"

"Let's start with the good news. The results from our follow-up Stock Take are in, and Dave and I have reviewed them. The percentage of

> Schedule a re-evaluation of where you really are in terms of demonstrating the behaviours that will manifest in the desired workplace culture. Repeat the Stock Take exercise for the KCAs you initially decided to focus on, share the results, and establish new goals. Do this regularly!

positive responses to the lead-in sentences has improved substantially. For instance, 'Around here, customers are...' went from fifty-six percent positive to seventy-two percent positive, and 'Around here, people are treated...' went from twenty-nine percent positive to sixty-four percent positive. But that's as much as you're going to find out right now."

"So what's the bad news?" I asked.

"Well," she said, "we're planning an all-company party to celebrate the return of our biggest customer, Drillco—their CEO is dropping by to show his support for what he calls 'the new partnership.' And I just realised that you're not going to be able to attend that party."

This took me by surprise. "Why not?"

"Because it's on your anniversary, Bruce," she said, smiling, "and I've gotten you and your wife tickets and reservations so you can spend the next two weeks in Honolulu. The plane leaves tomorrow night, which, it turns out, is the day before your anniversary. I don't want you missing that freaking flight."

She handed me an envelope. I opened it and checked the dates.

"You're right, Helen," I said. "It does look like an unresolvable scheduling conflict."

"So here's what we're going to do to deal with this problem," Helen announced, all business.

"You're getting your butt out of this building. You're heading home. You're telling your wife about the flight and the hotel accommodations. You're taking tomorrow off. And then you're getting to the airport with plenty of time to spare. Got it?"

"Got it," I said.

"Now get out of here," she ordered, grinning widely.

Long story short: I made my flight. On the plane, about half an hour after takeoff, I caught a glimpse of the back of someone's head. It looked dangerously similar to Sam's head: thinning white hair, evidence of glasses, frequent nodding. Astonished, I got out of my seat, walked down the aisle, and tried, tactfully, to confirm exactly who was sitting two rows ahead of us.

No doubt about it. It was him.

Sam was seated next to a very tense-looking businessman of about forty-five. The fellow was staring out the window purposefully, striving with all his might not to notice Sam.

I heard a familiar voice say, "Around here, we think positive and look for solutions. Is that a deal?"

The guy in the window seat looked first at Sam—this strange elderly seatmate of his who refused to disappear or shut up—and then at me, the total stranger lurking inexplicably in the aisle, staring at him. The poor guy looked, for all the world, like he'd been sealed inside a bad dream.

I remembered that feeling. I chuckled. Sam looked up at me, smiled, and then turned his gaze back toward his new number one prospect.

"So is it a deal?" he asked calmly.

"Go ahead and tell him yes," I said. "You won't regret it."

LIKE TO LEARN MORE?

IF THE UGRs CONCEPT AND processes outlined in this book resonated with you and you would like to use the concept to transform your culture, Stef and Steve have created a number of resources that can help.

At the book's web site – www.acultureturned.com - you'll find additional resources. You will also see details about how Steve and Stef can train internal Culture Champions (often called UGRs Champions) as well as training accredited UGRs Consultants.

Of course, as seasoned and expert conference presenters, Stef and Steve can be booked to speak at your event to help light the spark for genuine and lasting culture change.

Printed in Great Britain
by Amazon

49792054R00108